Six Highways to Home

A Cycling Journey from Whitehorse to Victoria

John Crouch

Chickadee Press
Victoria, BC

LIBRARY AND ARCHIVES CANADA CATALOGUING IN PUBLICATION

Crouch, John, 1941–, author
Six highways to home : a cycling journey from Whitehorse to Victoria / John Crouch.

ISBN 978-0-9731913-5-6 (pbk.)

1. Bicycle touring—Yukon. 2. Bicycle touring—British Columbia. I. Title.
GV1046.C3C76 2014 796.6'4097191 C2014-901366-3

Cover and book design: Frances Hunter
Maps: Amy Rutherford
Photographs: John Crouch collection

Cover photograph: Banks of Cayoosh Creek, southwest of Lillooet
Back cover photograph: South of Jade City, Northern British Columbia

Chickadee Press
303 – 1137 View Street
Victoria, BC Canada
V8V 3L9

— For Richard —

Acknowledgements

There are so many people to whom I am thankful it seems unfair to single anyone for special thanks. Everyone mentioned in this book contributed, in some fashion, to its realization. I am grateful to them all.

But there are exceptions. I am, once again, grateful to Frances Hunter for her design aesthetic. I have worked with Frances for many years and she always impresses with her thoughtful and creative approach to my books. The maps are Amy Rutherford's. They might look simple but they are not. Amy's renditions are perfect additions to the text. My good friend, Brian Connon, has been my faithful proofreader and occasional editor. I thank all three.

I was fortunate to have three sponsors for my journey: Mountain Equipment Co-op, Capital Iron and Team Sales, both of Victoria. I thank them for their assistance.

Parkinson Society of BC was very helpful in calming my anxiety about fundraising and in facilitating accommodation along my route. Thank you.

Apart from my wife, my daughter Mia is my biggest supporter. Her spirited approach to life never fails to infect and encourage me in whatever exploit I attempt. Thank you Mia.

To my wife, Lorinda, go my biggest thanks. Her patience and her unfailing love and support are the indispensable pillars of my wanderlust.

Leaving Whitehorse on July 12, 2011.

CONTENTS

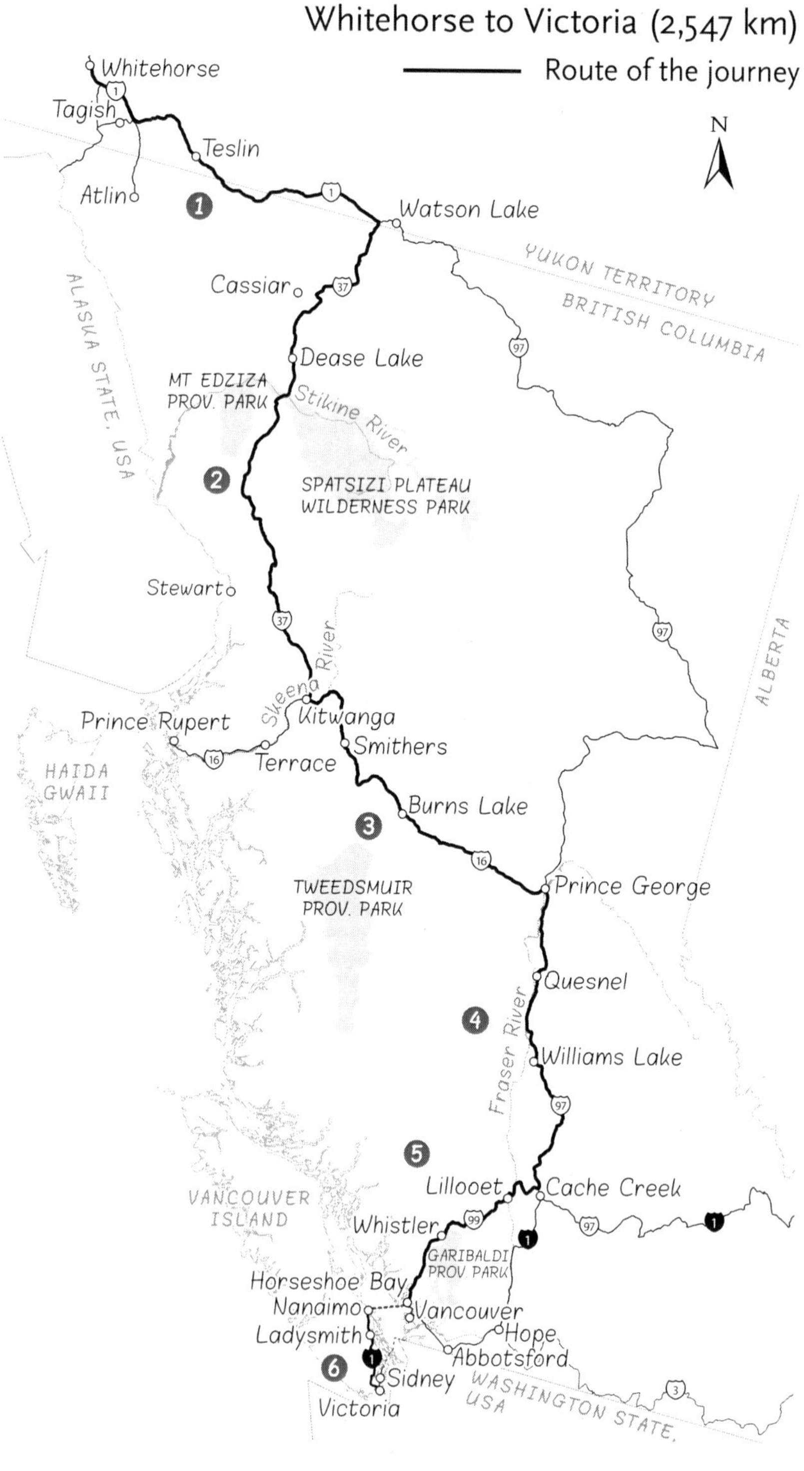
Whitehorse to Victoria (2,547 km)
Route of the journey
N
Whitehorse
Tagish
Teslin
Atlin
1
Watson Lake
YUKON TERRITORY
BRITISH COLUMBIA
Cassiar
37
ALASKA STATE, USA
Dease Lake
97
MT EDZIZA PROV. PARK
Stikine River
2
SPATSIZI PLATEAU WILDERNESS PARK
Stewart
37
97
Skeena River
ALBERTA
Kitwanga
Prince Rupert
Smithers
Terrace
16
HAIDA GWAII
Burns Lake
3
16
Prince George
TWEEDSMUIR PROV. PARK
Quesnel
4
Fraser River
Williams Lake
97
5
Lillooet
Cache Creek
VANCOUVER ISLAND
Whistler
99
97
1
GARIBALDI PROV PARK
Horseshoe Bay
Nanaimo
Vancouver
Hope
Ladysmith
Abbotsford
6
Sidney
Victoria
WASHINGTON STATE, USA
3

Prologue

In the summer of 2011 I cycled over 2,500 kilometres from Whitehorse in the Yukon to my home in Victoria on the southern tip of British Columbia's Vancouver Island. The journey took me a little over three weeks.

Choosing to ride my bike solo down the length of my home province was not a difficult decision. I'd wanted to do such a ride for the past 15 years. Now that I'd just turned 70 I thought it about time to put my feet where my mouth was—if you know what I mean. It would be both a personal odyssey in celebration of becoming a septuagenarian and a fund-raiser for Parkinson Society British Columbia. My ride would be a combination of a selfish goal and an attempt at doing something for someone other than myself.

Darkening the whiteness of paper with words that would transform my journey into a tale worth reading I knew would be a challenge. You see, nothing extraordinary happened, nothing extreme, nothing terrible or dangerous befell me as

I rode, mostly alone, along the white lines of the six highways I travelled on my journey south. Had I been mauled by a bear, hit by a truck, lost on an abandoned logging road or been on the receiving end of any of a myriad catastrophes—major or minor, I might have a riveting story to recount (assuming I was alive to write it). But nothing dreadful occurred.

Occasionally, in the weeks before I began my trip, a friend or acquaintance would ask, when I explained where I was going and what I was doing, "Will you write a book about it?" My response was, "No. It's not an unusual thing to do. And besides, it's not *that* far." (In the world of adventure cycling, my ride was nothing out of the ordinary. It's a journey thousands of people, young and not so young, have made before me.) I soon realized that for many, what I said was an understatement. For them it *was* an unusual thing and the distance *was* far. And, to make my journey even more unusual in their eyes, was the fact that I was doing it as a 70-year old. I began my journey with no intention of writing about it (for the public that is) apart my personal journal. Yet, as each day passed, pedalling south, what I saw, what I thought, the people I met, the places I stayed, what I was curious about—I slowly dared to acknowledge, dared to contemplate, might become the material of a book.

Once I accepted my experiences were worth writing about; once I had reconciled the perception, by others, that my journey was out of the ordinary with my own truth that it was not so unusual nor daunting, I knew I had a narrative that would give the reader a taste of what it was like to pedal a heavy bike day after day in a world much different from the one most of us inhabit most of the time.

My belief that we are never too old to embrace an adventure was a great incentive for me to embark on my journey and gave me the audacity and tenacity to complete it. All my adult life I've trained my body and my mind to race, climb, hike and to ride my bike. I didn't have to do anything special to prepare myself for the long ride from Whitehorse to Victoria. Training, competing, challenging my body and mind is what I love to do. And that's the secret: to do what you love to do—with a quiet intent, constant resolve and true passion—is one of life's simpler and immensely satisfying pleasures.

The aphorism, "It's the process, not the outcome" has only partial meaning in the context of my adventure. I wanted and needed to get home—the outcome. But the process—my journey, was what inspired me, fed me and helped me appreciate the largeness, the rawness, the grandeur and, always, the marvellous diversity of the province I live in.

Whitehorse to Nugget City (420 km)

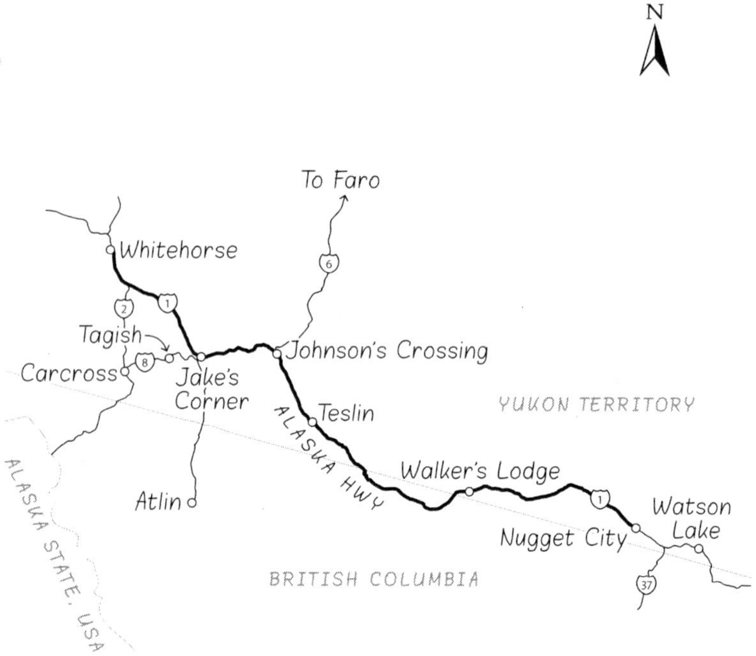

1 The Alaska Highway
Whitehorse to Nugget City

Whitehorse

A kilometre out of Whitehorse I was already breathing too hard. I'd found my first hill—the long climb up to the Alaska Highway that a few years ago planners decided should bypass the town. I shouldn't have been surprised. With many riverside settlements the roads in and out are often precipitously steep. It's what every cyclist comes to know and accept. Why would Whitehorse, ensconced on the banks of the Yukon River, be any different? Exactly! was the point I made to myself. Better get on with it. When the road calmed down and my breathing with it, I settled into an easy rhythm and began to wonder what the days would hold as I pedalled my way back to Victoria—my home.

It usually happens when I begin a longish ride or hike into an area I'm not familiar with, a slightly neurotic mixture of anticipation and trepidation creeps over me—rather like going on a blind date. This time I was dragging up my old nemesis—the What-if syndrome: What if the weather is really crappy all the time? What if I have a run-in with an aggressive bear? What if I'm hit by a truck? What if my body or my bike falls apart? What if... These and other negatives swirled around in my mind before I took that deep breath and said to myself, "Crouch, you've gone through this before. Now relax! You're going to have a great time no matter what the gods decide to throw at you." With that settled, I started to feel the warmth of the sun on my arms and my legs turning loose circles on the pedals. I rode on and began to consume the mountainous land that surrounded me. I was on my way.

I arrived in Whitehorse by plane from Victoria on a warm and sunny afternoon in mid-July 2011. Meeting me at the airport was Vanora Millar—an acquaintance I'd first met ten years previously at a workshop in Victoria. I remembered her as being very enthusiastic and friendly—easy to talk to. When I told her that, one day, I would ride my bike from Whitehorse to places south she immediately became excited by the prospect of my visiting her hometown. At the end of the weekend workshop she gave me her business card and said she'd love to play host and introduce me to the town whenever I showed up. Now, ten years hence, we were both holding true to our word. I had to admit I could no longer remember what Vanora looked like and told her so in our last phone conversation before I left home. She laughed and said she'd be responsible for greeting me at the airport. After all, she pointed out, there wouldn't be too many men with a white beard wrestling a bike box getting off the plane.

I'd disassembled my hybrid bike at home and packaged it into a sturdy cardboard bike box. The beauty of a bike box is you can cradle the frame, handlebars and wheels in between all sorts of things that you'd rarely suspect were in there like my tent, sleeping bag, Therm-a-Rest, clothes, even my dehydrated food. This left my two panniers light and, strapped together, went onto the plane as one piece of luggage. I spent the early afternoon on Vanora's back patio reassembling the bike and then set off for a test ride through the town with Vanora playing tour guide.

Vanora stuck out her left arm after we rode across the Lewes Boulevard bridge to turn onto the main road heading south out of town. "Robert Service Way" read the large overhead sign as we swung left. "What could be more Whitehorse-ish than that?" I called out. "Yes. And what about this?" She was pointing to the beached SS Klondike on the riverbank. It's a large white sternwheeler in immaculate shape (so it should be as a national historic site) and had carried freight between Whitehorse and Dawson City from 1937 to 1950 on the Yukon River. The only freight it sees now is summer tourists like me having their photograph taken leaning on its gunwales. But back to Robert Service. Apart from his two fictional characters, Sam McGee and Dan McGrew, he's the most famous of all Yukon residents. He was a lowly bank clerk when he arrived in Whitehorse in 1903 and by the time he left ten years later he was a renowned poet. Riding back towards town I was wracking my mind trying to remember whether it was "The Shooting of Sam McGee" and "The Cremation of Dan McGrew" or vice-versa. It was vice-versa.

Walking through Whitehorse's downtown the following afternoon after interviews with the CBC and two local newspapers, there seemed little doubt it was a government town. Logos of federal and territorial departments seemed everywhere—on the sides of office buildings, on their doors. It's not surprising that of the almost 35,000 residents of the Yukon, a little over 26,000 live in this one place. By urban standards it's a small town but it has the feel and look of a much larger place. Down by the riverbank is the impressive-looking Yukon Legislature Building—all metal-clad and modern. And at the north end of town the Yukon Arts Centre and the Canada Games Centre Multiplex are imposing enough to grace any town or city many times larger. But, whether small or large, every town has to have a primo coffee shop and bakery—preferably in the same location. Fitting the bill in Whitehorse, at the butt-end of Main Street, I found the Baked Café. Sitting outside sipping my decaf, I was impressed by the ambiance and the young, laid-back crowd. Not bad for a government town, I thought.

Leaving the café I spotted a young guy straddling a laden touring bike by the curb.

"Hi. Where you coming from?" I asked walking up to him.

"From Prudhoe Bay up in Alaska. You haven't seen a couple on touring bikes have you?" He said, looking up the street. I recognized instantly his broad Northeast England accent. He sounded like a Geordie—a native of Newcastle-on-Tyne (or there about).

"No, I haven't. You looking for them?

"Yes. We're travelling together. They're German and their English isn't that good so we kind of stick together." He looked down at the large face of his wristwatch. "They went off to find a grocery store. I told them I'd meet them here, by the café, in an hour. I'm not sure they'll find where it is. They're a bit late."

I wanted to ask if the Germans might have difficulty understanding his thick English accent but I didn't. I asked about his bike instead, how it was standing up to his trip.

"Oh, it's good so far." Then with a "Perhaps I should go

and look for them. We've got to find somewhere to camp yet. So long!" he pedalled off.

I was surprised by his rushing-off. I'd wanted to talk more; ask him questions about his trip; where he was headed. But he was gone.

Like most of the Yukon's modern history, Whitehorse got its start during the glory days of the late 1890's Klondike Gold Rush. The first prospectors came trudging up from the Alaska Panhandle through Skagway on the Chilkoot Trail. Soon, when the rush was really on, hordes of them came by steamship on the Yukon River. They would use White Horse (as it quickly become known) as a campground-stop on their way to the Klondike River and Dawson City, the epicentre of the Gold Rush. It was an ideal spot to rest and recoup after what would have been an alarming and exhausting journey through the churning rapids just to its south and the Miles Canyon beyond. For some poor guys, the journey to their fortune ended there, as many boats were lost to the raging waters.

Of course, the miners weren't the first to find the place useful. For millennia First Nations had used the flat riverside bank as one of their seasonal fishing camps. But it was these rapids that gave the fledgling settlement its name. In the minds of some of those early campers the white spume the rocks created as the river poured over them were images of the flaring manes of speeding white horses. The name stuck although, today, you'd be hard pressed to see what the fuss was about. Since 1958 those white-maned rapids have been tamed and are submerged beneath the waters of Schwatka Lake—a reservoir built by damming the Yukon River to provide electricity to the area. A prosaic ending to a poetic beginning, you might say. In 1953 the city became the capital of the territory and its name officially contracted from White Horse to Whitehorse in 1957.

DAY 1 Whitehorse to Jake's Corner

I had decided my first day on the road should be a bit shorter than my proposed 100-plus kilometres a day routine. By my calculation, the distance between Whitehorse and my day's destination at Jake's Corner was 90 kilometres. Travelling at an average speed of 15 kilometres an hour, I'd be there in a little over six hours—given the occasional break. I wanted a ride that would ease my body into the rigours of a long, continuous journey. I'd left Vanora's home just after 8 a.m. to take advantage of the cooler morning hours. She'd accompanied me to the "Welcome to Whitehorse" sign on the edge of town where we said our goodbyes. I thanked her profusely, of course, and told her that I couldn't have wished for a better host—helpful and accommodating while giving me lots of space. I'd enjoyed my three-day stay. On parting, I jokingly told her I would name my ride the V2V—the Vanora's to Victoria—in honour of her generosity. We laughed at the alliteration.

Out of town the Alaska Highway is relatively flat as it runs alongside the out-of-sight Yukon River somewhere on my left. In every direction all I could see was a great expanse of trees, valleys and mountains—a stunning panorama that I'd only ever seen in magazine and coffee-table book photographs. I was moved by the magnificence, the rawness and the silence of it all. My months of planning had finally set me amidst one of the special places in the whole of North America. I eventually crossed the Yukon as it flowed from the slender, 30 kilometre-long Marsh Lake.

What traffic there was flew by. I smiled the smile of satisfaction knowing my uncomplicated, human-powered vehicle made me as self-sufficient as I could be. Cars, trucks, RVs might be faster and more comfortable I thought, but I revelled in the simple pleasure of having all that I needed for my journey packed in my two panniers—my food, my clothing, my bed, my kitchen. They held the spare parts and tools for my bike, my money, my journal and a copy of Colin and Julie Angus's book *Rowed Trip.*

At noon I stopped at a beach access on the lake for lunch. In the distance I could see the volcanic cone-peaked Mount Lorne, a 2,020-metre (6,629-ft) beauty off to the southwest with snow still on its higher slopes. Although it was noontime the sun was still not high in the sky, its arc slinking across the horizon.

After Marsh Lake I'd have nothing more to do with the Yukon River, which was a shame because it's one of North America's great rivers (actually, the name "Yukon" means "great river" in Gwich'in, the First Nation language of the people who inhabit much of that part of the world). It flows in an enormous westerly crescent from its headwaters in British Columbia's Atlin Lake, through the Yukon and Alaska to its mouth in the Bering Sea, 3,190 kilometres away. The early afternoon became hot and despite trying to keep well hydrated and nourished I began to feel uncomfortable. (I learned that evening that the temperature had reached 30°C.) I'm not fond of hot weather (a good thing if you're from a west coast marine climate like I am) and was not yet acclimatized. Luckily, a southeast wind started to blow, which helped to cool me down, and I felt much better.

Rounding a sweeping left-hand bend I saw the outline of a cluster of buildings a few hundred metres ahead on the left. I checked my bike computer. It read 82 kilometres. This can't be

Jake's Corner yet, I told myself. I've got another eight kilometres to go. But it was. I'd miscalculated the day's ride. As I got closer I noticed a cyclist riding towards me on the opposite side. He saw me and crossed over to my side of the road.

"Hi, I'm Andy. You just come from Whitehorse?" He was a young, olive-skinned guy with a wide smile on his face even as he spoke.

"Yes. You heading there?

"No. I've just come up from Carcross but I thought you might have bumped into a British guy named Brian in Whitehorse or passed him on the road. That's why I asked. I'm heading east myself but I'm trying to hook up with guys that I know are heading this way."

I told him that I'd met a Brit the previous day in downtown Whitehorse who was touring, but no, I hadn't seen him on the road. Andy was riding a Surly touring bike with front and back panniers. He'd left Prudhoe Bay on the Alaskan shores of the Beaufort Sea 1,300 kilometres to the northwest almost a month earlier and was riding down to Seattle. He told me there was a cluster of riders heading south—a German couple (who Brian was accompanying), two Swiss guys, four Mexicans, a Korean and a Frenchman. It seemed quite the convoy. Andy knew all their names, where they were from and where they were heading. After we'd chatted a few minutes, he knew my name and destination too. Drawing a pint-sized laptop from his rear pannier he asked me for my email address. I chuckled and said, "Sorry Andy, the only computer I have is on my desk at home."

"How about a cell phone number?"

"Don't have one of those either."

"I guess we'll have to rely on bumping into each other on the road then"

With that, we said goodbye, he going toward Whitehorse

in search of Brian and the Germans, while I rode up to Jake's Corner.

Jake's Corner is what you might call a minimalist truck stop. It consists of a two-pump gas bar and a café-cum-restaurant, both looking winter-worn and in need of some TLC. Riding across the potholed gravel forecourt I made straight for the pumps. A couple of months earlier I'd phoned the owner of the place to ask about accommodation. (There was nothing on the websites I'd visited that indicated a campground or motel. All I could scrounge up was a phone number.) Her name was Joanne. She confirmed there was nowhere to stay at Jake's Corner. But, she added, I'd be welcome to pitch my tent behind the restaurant if I was stuck. I said I'd probably take up her offer. Terry would be the guy to see if I arrived during the day, she said, otherwise she and her husband would be working the pumps after 5 p.m.

Just as I was leaning my bike against the gas bar shelter a short, rotund man immerged wearing a floppy hat and a stubbly beard.

"You must be Terry." I said by way of greeting.

"Yup."

"Joanne said I could camp here for the night and you'd tell me where to go."

"Anywhere back there. Behind those tanks." He pointed to a slight embankment behind two tall rusty, white storage tanks about twenty metres away. As I looked in the direction he was pointing he obviously caught some anxiety on my face. He continued: "And don't be worried about any bears or cougars or foxes being 'round here. They're way up there, on White Mountain, and won't bother you none." He'd half turned and gestured to a high ridge no more than a kilometre away. "They got plenty to eat up there."

I walked my bike to the tanks and propped it against the skeletal remains of an old truck. There was a slight incline up to a flat area—evidently a graveyard for discarded kitchen and other equipment judging by the old freezer, giant mixer and bits of car engines and axles scattered among lengths of rusting metal roofing. I spotted a clear, level area next to the freezer and deemed it adequate for my small two-person tent. After setting-up camp I went in search of my favourite after-ride treat—a cold beer and potato or tortilla chips—at the restaurant. The young woman who served me was friendly and had an air of competence. I wondered what drew her to want to work in such an out-of-the-way place. In our brief conversation she told me she lived with her partner in Tagish, a First Nation community 18 kilometres to the south on the Carcross Road. When she wasn't working at the restaurant she spent her time gardening. In the winter, she and her partner drive south in their VW camper. She liked the lifestyle, she said.

Next to the washrooms I'd noticed a shower-room. Its door was locked but its sign read: "$5 Key at front counter." Great, I thought. Middle of the afternoon with hardly anybody around. Good time for an unrushed shower. The young woman gave me the key and a thick, white towel. She said she'd just cleaned the room and told me to "enjoy!" Although "salubrious" might not be the right word to describe the shower-room, in contrast to the rest of the building, it was pretty apt. Changed and refreshed I walked back to my tent and hung my washed riding gear on the branches of a sapling aspen.

Being too hot to snooze in my tent and no shade to speak of in the "graveyard," I took my book and went and sat on the covered porch at the end of the restaurant. There were at least a half dozen touring bikes leaning against the side of the building. Inside I could hear banter in thick English accents. They must be part of the convoy Andy was looking for, I thought, although I couldn't see him or his bike. The riders came outside in dribs and drabs. The Korean was easy to identify, as were the four Mexicans. I assumed the two white guys were the Swiss. Brian the Brit and the Germans were nowhere to be seen. By the time I was ready to chat they were on their bikes and moving off across the uneven gravel. They'd obviously given Jake's Corner a pass as a place to camp. I heard one of the Swiss shout "Johnson's Crossing" to the Korean as the group rode away. They had another 25 kilometres yet to ride.

After supper I walked down to the gas bar to thank Joanne for letting me camp overnight. While I was at it I would ask who was the Jake in Jake's Corner. I was curious. She wasn't there but her husband Phillip was and Terry was still hanging around. Between the two of them I got a very sketchy story of a grumpy and sometimes crazy American army engineer nicknamed Jake who was in charge of building a section of the Alaska Highway during the Second World War. He'd created a camp on the present site of the gas bar and supposedly pushed his men to incredible feats of endurance. That was as much as they knew. A more official story (which is only slightly more enlightening) is in R. C. Coutt's book *Yukon Places and Names*. He writes: "In 1942 the US Army Engineers set up a construction camp here under the command of Captain Jacoby (or Jackobsen) to build this section of the Alaska Highway and a cut-off to Tagish and Carcross for the Canol Pipeline. In 1949–50 a highway south to Atlin, BC, was built from here." What I've also found out is a much more intriguing, bizarrely coincidental and tinged-with-tragedy story of Jake's Corner.

Two months after my trip I emailed the Yukon Government's information centre asking for more details of Jake's Corner. This is the gist of a very personal reply from a government employee: In 1952 the employee's father, Roman Chaykowsky, bought a lodge 10 kilometres west of Jake's Corner. He'd come to Canada from the Ukraine after the war to work in the mines around Atlin, BC. A year after buying the lodge he watched in horror as his three-year-old daughter was struck and run over by a vehicle. Her death exacerbated an already troubled mind—during the war he had been conscripted into the German army and forced to witness the atrocities of a concentration camp. Then in 1961 the lodge he'd worked so hard to make a success burned to the ground. The building was not insured. Feeling the need to start afresh he bought land at Jake's Corner and built a new lodge he named the Crystal Palace. During the construction of the lodge the locals started to shorten his surname Chaykowsky to Jake—a name he kept until his death in 1994. His daughter (my correspondent) wrote, "My father had a reputation of being a madman to those who did not know him. He was a tortured soul." Hearing Phillip and Terry's version of Jake and reading the daughter's story, I thought it not too difficult to conjecture how a curmudgeonly American soldier and a troubled Ukrainian immigrant might become fused into one character in the folk-lore of the southern Yukon.

DAY 2 Jake's Corner to Teslin

Trundling my bike with its 62 lbs of gear carefully packed into and atop the rear panniers and handlebar bag down the embankment, I mounted and made for the smoother surface of the road. I could see three figures riding ahead of me. Catching up to them I recognized one of the two guys as the Brit I'd bumped into outside the Baked Café in Whitehorse. He and the couple riding with him, I assumed, were Brian and the Germans Andy had referred to. We all stopped and nattered for a minute or two—swapping names and our day's destinations. This, I came to realize, was one of the rituals of the road among the bike-touring fraternity. Brian had that weathered look of being on the bike for weeks on end with his tattooed arms, legs and neck melding into the smidgens of exposed sun tanned flesh. I asked where they'd stayed the night—not having seen them at Jake's Corner. They'd camped on the side of the road at the Atlin/Carcross junction across from Jake's Corner. Judging by their heavily loaded front and back panniers, they'd be riding at a much slower speed than me. We parted saying we'd probably see each other that evening at Teslin, 100 kilometres away.

Johnson's Crossing is a tiny settlement where the Alaska Highway crosses the Teslin River as it drains from the 120 kilometre-long Teslin Lake. Its locally famous bakery is attached to the spacious and tidy campground west of the long bridge spanning the river. It was an ideal spot for me to get a snack and a Coke knowing there'd be nothing until I hit Teslin. Walking through the bakery door I saw Andy eating breakfast. He hadn't met up with "the convoy" the previous day but knew they were heading for Johnson's Crossing. This is where he'd camped the night. Although they hadn't showed at the campground he thought they'd stayed at Squanga Lake—a government campsite a few kilometres before Johnson's Crossing. He was having a late start hoping he'd reconnect with some of the group.

Heading out the door the woman who had served me

followed and asked if I was the John who was riding from Whitehorse to Victoria as a fundraiser for Parkinson's disease. I told her yes, it was me. Having overheard me talking with Andy she thought I might be the one. She'd read about my trip in the Whitehorse Daily Star the previous day and wanted to know more about my ride and how she could donate. We chatted for quite a while about my journey and how it came about that my ride had morphed from a purely personal challenge into raising money for Parkinson Society British Columbia and creating awareness of the disease itself. The story I recounted went something like this:

One of my favourite phone conversations happens on Christmas Day when I speak with my family in England. It's usually late afternoon their time and they're recovering from their traditional midday meal. In 2010, as my sister passed the phone to Richard, my nephew, I sensed something was not quite right. His greeting was subdued. He was quieter than usual—reluctant to engage in conversation. He sounded slightly disoriented—unlike the Richard I'd seen the previous summer. I got off the phone knowing something had changed. You see, Richard has Parkinson's disease. He's been suffering from its progressive ravages for the past seven years, starting just after his 34th birthday.

For many years Richard had worked as a buyer for a major British shoe retailer. As the disease progressed, the medications he was on began seriously to affect his work and lifestyle. He gained weight, had difficulty sleeping, could no longer play soccer or go hiking. In short, he lost his usual zest for life. Counter intuitively as it seems, to mitigate the effects of his medications he took up photography (it was a creative response to his chronic sleeplessness—walking the streets of his hometown at 5 a.m. he saw much to photograph, from urban foxes and sunrises to early morning street life). After completing a course in photography he found a job with a photographic supply store. Eventually, the scourge of his disease forced him to the realization he could no longer hold a fulltime job. He's now a self-employed photographer supplementing his income with a small government disability benefit.

I've always been close to Richard even though we live far apart and that winter's phone conversation made me realize that the slippery slope of his Parkinson's had started to get steeper. I wanted to do something. Two months later, while I was making my final plans for my solo ride from the Yukon to Victoria, I decided to use the ride as my contribution to helping find a cure for this progressively debilitating disease.

We'd finished our conversation and I was about to leave when two riders pedalled towards me. They were the two Swiss guys. They had camped, as Andy had surmised, at the government campground a few kilometres back and were stopping for breakfast. Andy came out to join us and asked if they had seen the four Mexicans. They were still at the campground they said, and would be along soon. We were all heading for Teslin that day. We'd see each other there.

Riding to a stop in front of Teslin's Yukon Motel I could see Andy and another guy sitting on its veranda. Both had laptops in front of them and both were talking to each other while typing and then staring at their screens—multi-tasking, you might say. Andy had passed me soon after I'd left Johnson's Crossing and had arrived in Teslin early afternoon. The guy he was multi-tasking with was Nick, an Australian living in Canada who I'd get to know that evening. He'd been staying at the motel's campground for three days—partly to rest an injured knee and partly to deal with a reoccurring tire problem. He was riding from Anchorage to Penticton as training for an ultraman race he was competing in late August (a ridiculously arduous event in which competitors swim 10 kilometres, bike 420 kilometres and run 84 kilometres over three consecutive days).

Almost the first thing out of Andy's mouth was, " Have you seen anything of the four Mexicans? I wanted to tell him he was sounding repetitious; instead I told him the only cyclist I'd met after my lunch break was the Frenchman and he, I could see, was getting ready to leave the motel. The Frenchman, named Philippe, was young, fast and a loner and Andy thought we might not see him again. Andy would wait for the Mexicans and then, as planned, they'd all head to a cheaper campground ten kilometres further east. I began to think of Andy as a shepherd gathering and taking care of his flock.

Teslin is a small community on the eastern shores of Teslin Lake. Its 450 inhabitants are a mixture of Caucasian and First Nation people of the Tlingit tribe. The lake's name in the Tlingit language means "long narrow water." (Typical of First Nations, their names describe the essence of places, people, animals and things.) The Yukon Motel is on a small, sheltered bay on a stubbly finger of water that protrudes eastwards from the main body of the lake. The longest bridge on the Alaska Highway, the Nisutlin Bridge which traverses the bay's confluence with the lake, is less than 100 metres away. It's an interesting place to spend a peaceful night under a tent roof. Or so I thought.

The day had been hot again and I searched for a treed spot in the motel's campground. The few shaded sites were taken so I settled for a grassy flat area close to the lake with two large waterfront homes nearby. Nick's tent and bike were about fifteen metres away. Halfway through pitching my tent the two Swiss arrived and chose a site just behind me. We introduced ourselves more fully than at our morning encounter. They were from Bern; their names Christian and Adrian. They were riding from Anchorage to Vancouver via Vancouver Island. At 25 they thought themselves fit and young enough to complete the journey in less than six weeks. So far they were on schedule. Christian, the bearded one, unpacked a fishing rod and headed toward the lake. I left to go for my post ride treat—beer and chips—followed by a shower. When I got back, the Korean was installing himself nearby. For a diminutive guy, he had the most equipment I'd ever seen come off a touring bike. There was a huge two-person dome tent, a collapsible stool, a fancy camera with interchangeable lenses and a not-so-compact tripod. With his food, stove, sleeping pad and bag, his fully loaded bike must have weighed a ton. When he came over to talk I commented on his seemingly excessive load. He shrugged and said he was on a world trip and wanted to be comfortable. I guess when you're 28 you feel invincible.

I suggested to the Swiss and Lang, the Korean, that we go for a beer in the motel pub later in the evening. They thought it a good idea and agreed to meet there around eight. The heat of the day had cooled and the wind coming off the lake kept the mosquitoes reasonably at bay. From my picnic-bench dining table I could see dark storm clouds forming in the west. Before going to the pub I placed my panniers and cooking utensils and stove under the bench and made sure I'd left nothing lying around. I had hoped to spend the night without the fly on my tent (cooler that way) but the ominous clouds scotched that thought. With everything looking copasetic I left for the pub.

Nick was sitting with the two Swiss when I arrived. He had a newspaper open on the table.

"So you're famous I see." He was pointing to a full-page article about my ride in that day's issue of the Yukon News.

"Not really. I think they're desperate for news." Although I hadn't seen the article, I knew what he was referring to.

"Come on. Have you read this? 'Champion duathlete begins ride for Parkinson's'" he read out loud. " It says you won the world endurance duathlon championship in Holland ten years ago when you were sixty. That means you're seventy now, right?"

"Yes. But that was..."

"I'm goin' to keep a copy of this." He interrupted, as he tore the page out. "I thought I was the old guy around here, but man..."

I asked how old he was. He was 48.

Lang had joined us now and the five of us started talking about bike touring and how much we enjoyed being in "the nature" as the Swiss referred to wilderness. Nick had by far the most experience. He'd cycled throughout South America, his native Australia and across Canada. His compact and tautly muscular body seemed well suited to bike touring. Christian and Adrian talked about their jobs as engineers in Bern and how they had dreamed of cycling in North America since high school. Lang told a bizarre and amusing story of testing his bear spray in an Anchorage church hall full of people. A wry smile came on his face as he described how two burly guys, coughing and sneezing with tears running down their cheeks, ejected him from the place.

Nick and I swapped stories about our triathlon days. I'd competed in the 2005 Ironman Canada race in Penticton. He'd done the event the year previous to mine but had also done three others before that. We both know Steve King, the voice of Ironman Canada and countless other races, large and small, throughout North America. Like most people who've heard Steve commentate, we expressed our amazement at his encyclopedic knowledge of competitors' accomplishments—whether elite or weekend warrior. When an athlete crossed the finish line he'd rattle off their latest result, what they had achieved in their career, how old they were and where they lived. And this wasn't for a few, it was for thousands.

Before I left Victoria I agreed to phone my wife Lorinda and my daughter Mia every other day once I was on the road. Lorinda was doubtful that I'd find pay phones with such regularity but, if I were lucky, she'd be thankful to know I was still alive and pedalling. Mia was writing a Facebook page (I call it a blog) on my journey and needed to hear about my daily exploits. I left the group and went into the motel entrance to make the calls. Looking out the open door I could see a menacing sky. By the time I'd finished calling the rain had started and a thunderstorm was rolling across the lake. The others joined me on the veranda and watched the storm unfold. Minutes later forked lightning lit up the blackened sky followed by explosions of booming thunder. Hail and rain poured like a horizontal waterfall off the veranda roof onto the quickly flooding parking lot in front of us. The storm became a natural and spectacular *son et lumière* being performed in front of us—and we had grandstand seats. Who would be the first to run back to the tents? Nobody was inclined. We all knew we'd be soaked as soon as we stepped off the veranda. We'd wait. Wouldn't be too long before the storm petered out, we assured ourselves. No such luck.

We waited an hour-and-a-half for the pelting rain to ease and finally stop and then walked back to see what mischief had been caused. Lang's was the only tent that wasn't in water. For the rest of us, we saw our tents sitting in a huge pool that looked like an extension of the lake itself. My tent faired the worst. I hadn't closed the fly's flap-door and the rain had penetrated the mesh door of the tent itself. Fortunately, the lip of the door and the tent's waterproof flooring prevented the surrounding two-inch-deep water from flooding the whole thing. The two panniers I'd stuck under the table were floating in even deeper water. I looked at my tent again. If I crawled inside and depressed the floor I knew the water would come rushing in. There was no way I could sleep there. It was now ten-thirty and although the sun was not exactly setting the light was definitely dim. (The summer sun never really sets in the Yukon.) I knew the motel was full so I couldn't stay there. I turned and looked at the two houses I'd noticed earlier. One had a SUV in front and the lights were on downstairs. The second had no vehicle out front nor were there any lights on. I went and checked it out. A large porch covered the front door and there was a number two on the lintel. I peered through the windows. The rooms were furnished but didn't look lived in. Being so close to the motel I assumed they were rental homes. I went back to my tent and told the Swiss I was going to spend the night on house number two's front porch.

Carefully pulling my sleeping bag and Therm-a-Rest from the tent, I took them to the porch. I returned for the panniers. If it rained again during the night they wouldn't get any wetter. I had just settled into my bag when I heard children's voices. I sat up to see who they were and where they were going. There were four of them—not much older then nine or ten, and were walking to a shed by the driveway to the house were I was squatting. They were no more than a few metres away when one of them noticed me. He told me, rather apologetically, that they were retrieving a bike I could see leaning against the shed. As they took off, I realized I might be in trouble. There was no way the kids weren't going to tell some adult that a strange old man was sleeping on the porch of the house.

Five minutes later I heard, then saw, a large, late-model pickup truck with its headlights on high beam coming up the driveway and stop inches from the front steps to the porch. A tall guy jumped out and came striding up the steps toward me shouting, " What the fuck are you doing here? Get out." I was out of my bag in a flash. As soon as I was standing the guy recognized me. We had spoken with each other in the motel lounge during the storm about my trip and he'd suggested possible campgrounds I could stay at as I rode east. I'd assumed that he was the motel owner or manager by the way he spoke to the staff. Gathering up my things I explained about being flooded out of my tent. In a calmer tone he told me that the house was rented out and guests were due to arrive any minute. " You can't stay here. You gotta move fast." He was just about to grab one of my panniers when he said. "Wait here a minute, you can stay in the shed. Let me make some space." He ran over to the shed and went inside. I could hear him moving things around and then, appearing at the door, he called me over. "You should be okay in here. It's a bit smelly but it's dry." I sheepishly thanked him and stepped inside carrying my sleeping bag.

The place was rank with gas fumes. Pushed back against the walls was a jumble of boating paraphernalia—a couple of outboard motors, a collection of small fuel tanks, life jackets, tangled ropes, waterproof clothing and fishing gear. The floor was stained with oil but had obviously been quickly swept. As he drove away, I saw two children huddled next to him quizzically peering at me out the cab window. I went back to the porch and ferried the rest of my gear to the shed. I fell asleep hoping the morning would bring clear skies and a warm temperature.

Day 3 Teslin to Walker's Continental Divide Lodge

Not a bad night's sleep, I concluded, walking from the shed, sleeping bag over my shoulder and pad under my arm, to inspect my tent. The giant puddle had disappeared and the morning sun was drying things out. Nick, the Aussie, was already shaking his tent out and draping it next to his sleeping bag on the fence separating the lakeshore from the campground. The Swiss and Lang, the Korean weren't up yet. Although it was a little after six I knew I wouldn't be getting an early start. With my soggy tent and damp panniers, riding shoes, saddle and other gear to dry, I would have to wait at least two or three hours. After I had spread everything out on the surrounding rocks, picnic table and fence and had my breakfast of muesli and orange juice, I walked over to the motel to buy a cigarette lighter. Yes, a cigarette lighter. The one that I had was so wet it wouldn't light and was drying out with the rest of my stuff. Without a lighter I couldn't start my miniature butane stove and make myself a much-needed cup of coffee. It was a few minutes before 7 o'clock when I arrived at the motel's door. Through the glass pane I saw the outline of the person unlocking. It was the guy with the truck who'd turfed me off the porch a few hours earlier. He smiled as we exchanged our good-mornings. I apologized for my trespassing misdemeanor. "Don't worry about it," he said. "The renters didn't show up 'til gone midnight anyway." He sold me a lighter and we parted wishing one another a great day.

It was around ten o'clock when I eventually left the campground and rode to join the highway and cross the 500-metre-long Nisutlin Bridge on my way east. In this part of the Yukon, the Alaska Highway is a bold stroke across the mountainous terrain of the Yukon Plateau. It's a wide swath of asphalt that winds through broad, deeply-etched valleys, long, sinewy lakes, massive volcanic-formed peaks and swiftly flowing rivers and creeks. And there are trees—spruce, pine, aspen, birch; millions of hectares of trees everywhere. And the road slices through them all. Settlements are few and the distance between them determined where I'd end my day. The title of Rory Stewart's book describing his trek across Afghanistan in 2002, *The Places in Between,* came to mind months before my trip as I searched my map and plotted where I could camp or take a motel.

Andy, the shepherd, referred to the highway as the Alcan Highway—a contraction of Alaskan-Canadian Highway. It's the original name used from the beginning of construction in 1942 (although, there are some accounts of the road's history that give Pioneer Road as its first name). I'd never heard that name used before. Nowadays it's generally known as the Alaska Highway. Trying to imagine how such a road was conceived and then built, even from today's perspective, is difficult especially knowing it was constructed using technology and equipment of 70 years ago. Ironically, we can thank the Japanese for motivating the Americans to build it. If it weren't for their bombing of Pearl Harbour and therefore invading US territory in December of 1941, the road's construction might have been delayed for decades. As it was, the Americans were deathly afraid that the boldness of Japan's attack was a portent of their intention to infiltrate the whole of North America via Alaska. After all, it was only a little more than a stones throw away from Japan itself. Their worst fears were confirmed the following June—the Japanese struck at Alaska's Aleutian Islands.

The road's construction began in April of 1942 and took 11,000 US soldiers and 6,000 civilians only eight months and 12 days to finish it the following November—an incredible act of American bravura. While the lowly American recruit had no choice whether or not to work on the project, civilians did. The text of one of the recruitment ads describes, very bluntly, the working conditions they could expect: "Men hired for this job will be required to work and live under the most extreme conditions imaginable. Temperatures will range from 90 degrees above zero to 70 degrees below zero [they're talking Fahrenheit here]. Men will have to fight swamps, rivers, ice and cold. Mosquitoes, flies and gnats will not only be annoying but will cause bodily harm. If you are not prepared to work under these and similar conditions, do not apply." Seems that an adverse working environment deterred neither the soldiers nor the civilians from doing their job; in fact, it probably acted as a strong incentive to get the road finished in the shortest time possible. There were three staging points for the construction of the 2,288 kilometre-long (1,422 mile) new road: Dawson Creek, in northeastern BC, was its southern end; Whitehorse, in the Yukon, was roughly the middle and Delta Junction, in Alaska, was the end. Work crews started at each point and worked towards each other.

For the US army, the enormity of the task proved a turning point in its attitude toward black recruits. Until the Pearl

Harbour attack US military policy dictated that blacks could not be deployed in the north nor see active service anywhere. They even had their own "black" regiments (meaning, "segregated"). That all changed with the building of the highway. Troops were desperately scarce so blacks were shipped to northern BC, the Yukon and Alaska to work side by side with whites. Like everyone else who worked on the project they suffered from poor housing (living in tents mostly), were sleep deprived (working 20-hour days, seven days a week) and endured punishingly cold weather (-40°F for weeks on end). Though the majority were from the southern states, they persevered and, at the highway's completion, many were decorated for their service and sent to fight in the South Pacific and Europe. So much for segregation.

My morning's ride had hardly started when I recognized the name of the campground where Andy and the Mexicans had planned to stay. "Dawson Peaks" was etched on a large, artistically rendered sign of mountaintops at its entrance driveway. I decided to see if Andy and his friends had left yet. If they hadn't, it would be a good time to meet the Mexicans whom I'd already started to refer to as the "Four Amigos." True to form, even at 10:30 in the morning, they were still getting ready to leave. Andy introduced me as if they already knew who I was, where I was from and where I was heading. "This is John. You know, the guy I was telling you about." Over the next hour, as the six of us rode together, I got used to their names and managed to talk, one on one, with each of them. They were all from Guadalajara and had been friends since high school. Three of them: Louie, Pedro and Alex were the same age—21, while the fourth, Mario was 25. (They referred to themselves as the Three Musketeers and D'Artagnan, which seemed to me a fitting description as

Mario had been living in New York for the past year and just been reunited with the three for the trip.) Because of their late start they weren't ready to take lunch when I decided to. We were all heading for the same destination—Walker's Continental Divide Lodge, so we'd see each other there.

Stopping at an abandoned shack I found an open spot with a large rock to prop my bike against. I'd quickly remembered mosquitoes much prefer shaded areas such as trees and shrubs to the open—which was quite the opposite to a perspiring cyclist taking his lunch break. Before I settled into my cheese and crackers and orange juice (what a combination!) Christian and Adrian rolled up. They were ready for lunch but were going a kilometre or two up the road to a rest area beside the Morley River. Christian had heard it was a good place to fish. Would I join them? Yes, I would. Within fifteen minutes of Christian's piecing together his fishing rod, walking down the trail to the river, wading in thigh-deep and casting, he'd caught a superb, foot-long Arctic grayling. While Christian was gutting the fish and Adrian assembling and lighting the stove, Brian and the German couple arrived. They, I realized, were "boondockers," choosing to camp on the side of the road or on some vacant land than in an organized campground. That's why I hadn't seen them in Teslin. They'd camped near the long bridge, hidden from view. Brian had travelled south with Andy from Prudhoe Bay. But Brian had a much longer journey in front of him. Over two years, he was cycling his way down to Tierra del Fuego on the southern tip of Argentina. In these early stages of his trip he was being prudent with his cash—thus, his boondocking. I decided to leave the lunch group and start riding. It was already past one o'clock and I still had over 80 kilometres left to cover.

Soon after leaving Teslin that morning I'd encountered Nick repairing a flat on the side of the road. For some inexplicable reason (or Aussie logic) he'd chosen to use a regular road bike rather than a sturdier touring or hybrid bike to pull his compact, one-wheeled trailer. (To be truthful, his stated reason was that he wanted to replicate the kind of bike he'd use in his upcoming Ultraman race. Also, he wanted to be fast.) Consequently, his wheels were narrow and his tires thin. The road surface is, for the most part, a durable but rough chip-seal. (Chip-seal is gravel pressed or rolled into a bed of asphalt.) Nick's bike and the road surface were as incompatible as rollerblades and dirt. I don't know how many flats he'd had before I met him, but I know it was a major feature of his ride south. We chatted about his problem for a minute or two and then I left him—my offer of help declined and his attitude stoically positive.

About mid-afternoon I came across Nick again. He was on the roadside with his rear wheel in his hand. "How did you get here?" I asked. He said he'd past me while I was having lunch with Christian and Adrian at Morley River—he'd seen us from the road. Lying at his feet were about a half dozen inner tubes—most of which had black electrician's tape wrapped around some part of their circumference. He'd concluded it was the wheel's rim that was causing the problem so he was lining it with an unusable inner tube. I was impressed by his unperturbed state of mind especially as he'd run out of spare tubes. Of course, my tubes were too big to fit his wheel. Before I left him Lang came to a stop beside us. His tubes were of no use either so he tootled off. I imagined Nick would be putting his thumb out if his luck continued to desert him.

It was a perfect day for riding—clear skies, not too hot

and a following wind. Late afternoon I was passing through a long, undulating valley flanked by towering volcanic cones. I didn't know it, but I was crossing an ancient geological formation known as the Quesnellia Terrane. A terrane is a body of rock that is different in type and age from the surrounding material and, apparently, the mountain I was riding past on my right, the 2,173-metre (7,129-ft) Simpson Peak, was a good example of that phenomenon. Massive and implacable as the mountain seems to be, it represents the much diminished volcanic remains of a gigantic landscape that was formed between one and two hundred million years ago during the Jurassic period. It's still being whittled down by the erosive forces of nature and time to a fraction of its original size. Looking across the valley at the mountain peak I found it hard to comprehend that, in times past, it was many times larger. The roadside plaque that explained all this said it was named Quesnellia for the BC town of Quesnel where the terrane or distinctive volcanic rock was well exposed. (And where I planned to stop two weeks later.)

I eventually caught up to Lang and we played cat and mouse as I rode away from him on the significant uphills (including some 7 and 8%ers) while he, on his much heavier bike, caught and passed me on the downhills. We were, in fact, climbing the western slope of the Continental Divide that runs in a north/south direction across the BC-Yukon border. By the time we leaned our bikes outside the Walker's Continental Divide Lodge office I'd been pedalling for over seven hours and had covered 125 kilometres. That evening the speedier members of the convoy gathered around my picnic table to share the day's stories, the most important of which was that Nick had succeeded in repairing his wheel although he wasn't sure it would hold. A note of pessimism about his ability (or more accurately, his bike's) to complete his ride was nudging its way into his mind. About ten o'clock the Four Amigos, Nick and Andy went over to a scruffy volleyball court for a pickup game. I was flattered when they tried to cajole me into playing. "No, I'm not Superman," I quipped and crawled into bed. Lang was already in his tent. There was no sign of the Swiss or Brian the Brit and the Germans.

Day 4 Walker's Continental Divide Lodge to Nugget City

I woke to the splatter of rain on my tent. Not what I wanted. But it wasn't surprising either. The forecast in Whitehorse before I left was for a low-pressure system to overtake the area in the next few days and would create unsettled weather (some had said for the rest of the summer). I knew I needed to get up, break camp and be gone before my equipment and I got drenched again. It was six o'clock and I was the first one up. The rain was light and intermittent until I was ready to leave then it started to pour. I donned my raingear and covered my panniers with waterproof covers. I also tied a thick plastic bag over my non-waterproof handlebar bag—a good thing to do as it held my wallet and camera. It's not that I mind riding in the rain—like most cyclists, I've done it countless times (as I have with running and hiking), but it's the initial moment when you place your body into its uncomfortableness that I dislike. Once I experience the first drops, I'm fine (relatively). It's akin to standing on the edge of a frigid lake in your bathing suit and asking yourself if you really want to jump in.

The highway seemed narrower in the low clouds and

though I was riding through the Cassiar Mountains I could see none of them. I was thankful that the road's grade tipped slightly downward as I cruised through the wetness and off the Continental Divide. Often referred to as the Great Divide, the divide delineates the direction the watersheds of North, Central and South America flow. It follows a line that starts at Cape Prince of Wales, Alaska, the most westerly point of the mainland of the Americas and, through mostly mountainous terrain, zigzags its way down through western Canada and the US, through Central and South America to Patagonia and Tierra del Fuego in southern Argentina. From where I was riding in the southern Yukon the waters flowed either west to the Pacific Ocean or north to the Arctic Ocean depending on which side of the divide they were on. Yesterday, they flowed west; today, they flow north.

Bears played a big part of my pre-trip musings. All the years that I've been tramping about in the mountains of North America I've never come face to face with a bear. I've seen them from a distance and through my binocs (one monster grizzly in the North Cascades in Washington State). I've heard them moving through the underbrush, but no, never close up. I suppose the closest I've come to a grizzly was years ago when I was cycling through the Coast Mountains. At the bottom of Heckman Pass in Tweedsmuir Park in west-central BC, the Atnarko River passes close to the road. I'd read that there's usually a large concentration of grizzlies in that location especially when the chum salmon were running at the end of August—the time I was there. I stopped at the ranger station and asked if it was okay to camp in the nearby campsite. The ranger advised against it. He said there were more than a dozen eating their fill not a 100 metres away on the riverbank. I didn't stop to look. (Travelling on the ferry from Bella Coola to Vancouver Island two days later I'd met a small group of cyclists who'd stopped and actually camped by the river at that very spot. They saw many grizzlies but said they were too concerned with fishing than with bothering humans. Admitting to not a little apprehension, they trusted the notion of safety in numbers.)

I'd read the literature on bears—their behaviour and our behaviour in their presence. I'd bought my bear banger and bear spray ("bearscare" as one First Nation guy called it). I was prepared to make myself appear tall and create as much noise as I could and, although I hadn't practiced the fetal position yet, I would keep my whistle handy. I guess for someone who's essentially a city slicker like me it's not unusual to be a tad paranoid about having an encounter with either an *Ursus arctus horribilis* (grizzly bear) or a *Ursus americanus* (black bear). Months before my trip I had lurid visions of being mauled in my tent by a manic bear. Occasionally the visions would prevent me falling asleep at night. It wasn't until I finally convinced myself of the irrationality of such thoughts that I was able not to worry—and get to sleep with a tranquil mind.

It was just after I'd had my lunch and the rain had morphed into drizzle that I first saw him. The black bear was no more than 15 metres away grazing in the wide swath of tall grass off to the side of the road. I came to a stop and fumbled for my whistle. I needn't have bothered. He knew I was there. Rearing up on his hind legs he stood staring at me—tall, vigilant and intimidating. His black satin fur, though dulled by the rain, rippled as he moved. He was on my side of the road—or I was on his, depending on your point of view. I could feel the adrenalin surging through my muscles and my neck hair tightening. I looked behind to see if any traffic was coming. That might scare him off, I thought. No traffic.

I waited and waited hoping he would move into the bush. He held his ground, his small beady eyes firmly in my direction. I guess it was HIS side of the road. Okay, I'll move. Slowly I pedalled the six metres to the other side of the highway and rode past him. We both turned our heads keeping our eyes on each other. I was perhaps 20 metres on when he dropped back on all fours and resumed munching away on the slender grass. For him, I was a mere interruption. For me he was my first encounter with one of the princes of nature.

Apart from a brief stop at the Rancheria Resort café for an orange juice and get a respite from the rain, I spoke to no one until I reached the romantically-named Nugget City. (I could easily have written, "exaggeratedly-named" for as far as I can tell, there's never been any gold or other precious metal found on the site.) The place is a small resort with an assortment of cabins, a log-construction gift shop, a restaurant and a RV park and campground. It also had a row of prefabricated single bedrooms (motel style) tucked behind the geranium-clad cabins—which is where I spent the night and dried out. My room was nothing fancy—a bed with a table and chair squeezed between it and a windowless wall. I walked over to the Wolf It Down restaurant (not a place you're encouraged to linger over a well cooked meal tastefully presented, obviously) for my well deserved after-ride treat.

Out of the restaurant window I saw Andy and Lang arrive and proceed to drape their sopping tents over nearby railings. Over beers they described their late and wet start (even later were the Mexicans) and how Nick had postponed his departure until the weather improved. Andy said he'd lost touch with Christian and Adrian. And Brian and the Germans were nowhere to be found. I hadn't realized it at the time but the previous day's Morley River lunch-stop was the last I would see of the Swiss, the Brit or the Germans. I was beginning to understand one of the existential realities of bike touring. The remaining convoy agreed to rendezvous at the junction of Highway 37 and the Alaska Highway two kilometres west of Nugget City. They'd heard it was cheaper and even possible to tent for free behind the small store and gas bar.

After I'd cooked and eaten my supper I phoned Lorinda and Mia from the payphone adjacent to the Wolf It Down. Both had been skeptical about the availability of such "old technology," especially after my previous summer's solo bike trip in Washington State where payphones were hard to find. As with this trip, I'd preferred to be without a cell phone and I'd go days without talking to Lorinda. I was in Ellensburg on a quiet Sunday morning when I asked a city work crew to point me in the direction of a payphone. At first they thought I was after a morning newspaper (my Brit accent causing some auditory confusion), but when they understood what I wanted, they looked perplexed and confessed they didn't know of one. Now, in the Yukon, they seemed to be at every street corner—if you conceive street corners being at 100 kilometre intervals.

Lorinda and Mia were relieved I was on schedule and "safe and sound." (The latter adjective, as it applies to the mind, has always been a cause of dispute between Lorinda and me when discussing my enjoyment of being alone in the wild.) The story of my "bear encounter" provoked a few questions. "Were you frightened?" was one of them. I believe I detected some disappointment though when they realized how uneventful the occurrence had actually been. Our next conversation, I told them, would be in BC—home territory as it were, and on a completely different highway.

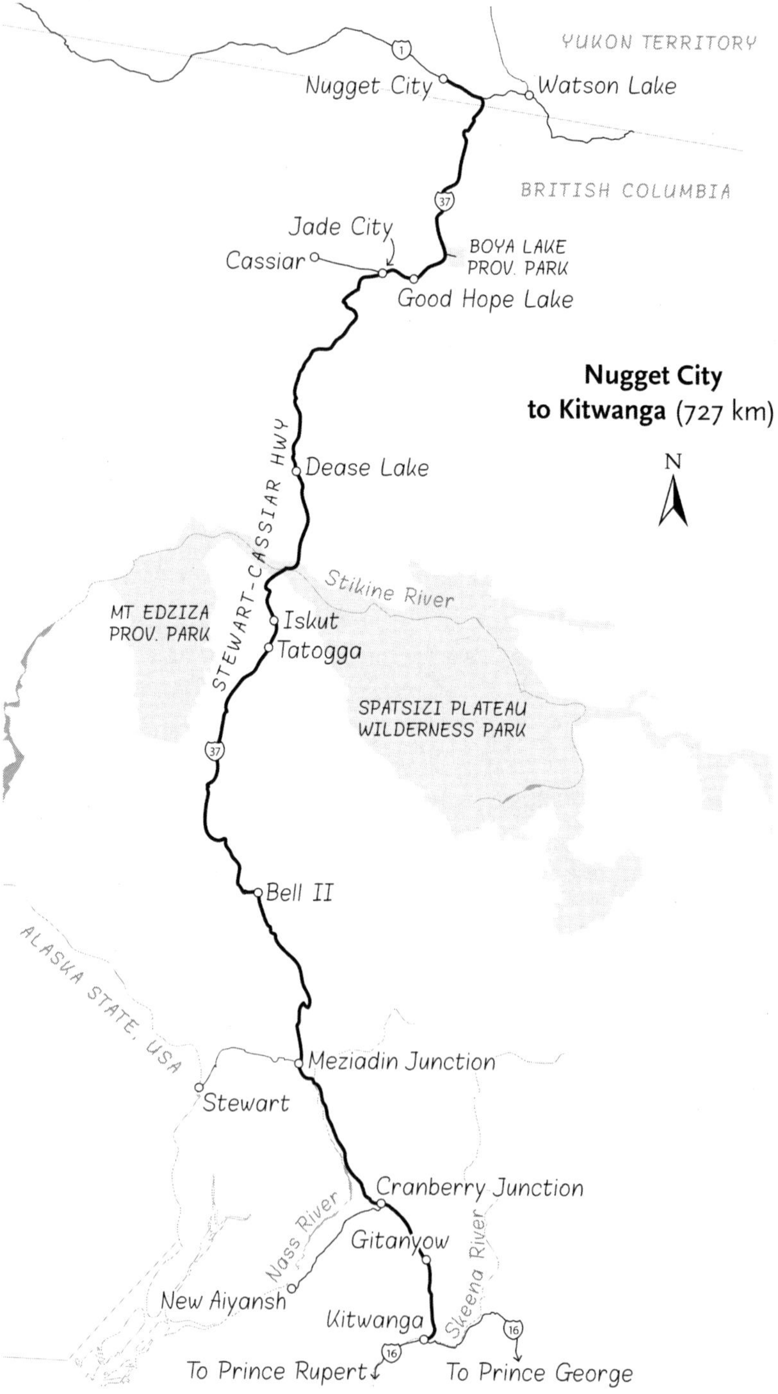

YUKON TERRITORY
BRITISH COLUMBIA
1
Nugget City
Watson Lake
37
Jade City
Cassiar
BOYA LAKE
PROV. PARK
Good Hope Lake
Nugget City
to Kitwanga (727 km)
N
STEWART-CASSIAR HWY
Dease Lake
Stikine River
MT EDZIZA
PROV. PARK
Iskut
Tatogga
SPATSIZI PLATEAU
WILDERNESS PARK
37
Bell II
ALASKA STATE, USA
Meziadin Junction
Stewart
Cranberry Junction
Nass River
Gitanyow
Skeena River
New Aiyansh
Kitwanga
16
16
To Prince Rupert
To Prince George

2 The Stewart-Cassiar Highway (Highway 37)
Nugget City to Kitwanga

Day 5 Nugget City to Boya Lake Provincial Park

It was 8:30 a.m. Andy and the now-depleted convoy were nowhere to be seen when I arrived at the store and gas bar at the junction of the Alaska Highway and Highway 37. They'd planned to spend the night here but when I asked the rather grumpy elderly couple who ran the place if they'd seen the small band of cyclists, the woman answered with a curt, "No." Back in the spring, when I was figuring out my itinerary, I'd considered this as a possible overnight stop. I was glad I'd chosen Nugget City. The place (simply called Junction 37 Services) looked run-down despite a large signage board extolling its services. Its buildings were sprawled over a large, treeless expanse of potholed gravel, although I could see an empty RV park and campground set among a grove of pines. Like umpteen other such operations in that part of the world, it was for sale.

Before I started my trip an acquaintance posed this rather rhetorical question: "And you'll have a cell phone won't you?" (I had others like it but less blunt.) While I understood the reasoning behind this question's oblique reference to safety and the peace of mind of those at home, and its implied irresponsibility if I didn't take one, my long answer would not be what they wanted to hear. For me, not wanting to take a cell phone is something akin to Edward Abbey's take on modern civilization's encroachment on the deserts of the southwestern US. In his book, *Desert Solitaire,* he mourns the diminution of natural places and the possibilities of finding pure solitude. I still have a hankering for the time before the cell phone, before the smart phone, when you went off into the mountains with little or no contact with anyone. It was a simple, "Goodbye. See you in three weeks." Leaving the security of home for places unknown demands a sense of self-sufficiency, of self-awareness and an understanding of the boundaries and limits of your own capabilities—physical and mental. Planning and preparation are vital. I've never gone into the wild without letting someone know where I'm going, who I'm going with and for how long. I've also never gone into the mountains or on a long bike trip without good maps, a first-aid kit, extra food, warm clothing, rain gear and spare cash.

Contentious as it may be, it seems oxymoronic to me to talk about being in the wilderness while having your cell phone in your back pocket—just in case. Admitted, there's wilderness and there's "wilderness." One is land that has been modified by our hands but still has many of the essential elements of its original wildness (a national park, for instance). We can intrude and revel in its awesome splendour. The other is a vastness that is almost impenetrable. It has little or no human intrusion. It's the former that I'm talking about. I've always luxuriated in being in the midst of the silence and beauty of this natural world with its taste of freedom, its slight whiff of danger as a kind of opiate (to paraphrase Abbey). When people contend that venturing into this wilderness without a modern communications device is reckless and thoughtless, they are dismissing the countless journeys and adventures humans have made and experienced throughout the ages as hedonistic, egotistical and a dereliction of responsibility.

There's no denying that travelling alone (or even with a friend, which I often do) into remote or semi-remote areas is, in essence, an act of selfishness. But it's also an act of discovery—of the landscape and of oneself. It's a desire to feel more complete, to be part of something that transcends the ordinariness of being human. Never is the intention to cause worry or concern for one's family or friends. If that were the overriding consideration we'd never set foot outside the door. So, my short (and usual) answer to a question like that is, "No, I won't be taking a cell phone with me. Besides," I'd add, trying to sound knowledgeable and not too facetious, "having one in remote areas, especially in the mountains, is useless because reception is either non-existent or very sporadic." That seems to mollify most enquirers.

Another question I was often asked was: "Are you taking a GPS?" Not to disparage those who asked this question, but it was clear they hadn't a clue about the geography of the Yukon and BC. My glib response was, "No need. It's simple. The route consists of three left turns and three right turns. I can't get lost." Which, when you look at the map, is essentially the truth. In slightly more detail, this is how I described my route: I'd take the Alaska Highway from Whitehorse to its junction with Highway 37—the Stewart-Cassiar and turn south. At the end of that 740-kilometre-long road, I'd turn east onto Highway 16—the Yellowhead—to Prince George. From Prince George I'd ride to just south of Clinton to take Highway 99 to Horseshoe Bay via Lillooet, Pemberton, Whistler and Squamish. I'd take the ferry to Nanaimo and then ride south on the Trans-Canada to Victoria. (One woman, after reading that I wouldn't have a cell phone with me, phoned me to suggest I take a SPOT—a small satellite GPS beacon that can tell people exactly where you are. I thanked her but said I'd be fine. I nearly added that my desire was not to be SPOTted—but I restrained myself.)

I wasn't long on my new highway when I came upon the convoy. They had stopped to visit a small group of First Nations mushroom pickers who'd set up a collection station on a wide clearing on the side of the road. In the short distance I covered that morning I'd noticed a car or truck parked on the side of the road every now and then and wondered why. I also saw that for kilometres in every direction the trees were dead. The previous summer there'd been an extremely large forest fire (35,000 hectares to be exact) along this stretch of highway that not only closed it and the Alaska Highway for a time but also could be seen a hundred kilometres away. Apparently, morel mushrooms grow and proliferate like mad in burnt spruce and pine forests. Now I realized who the vehicles belonged to—pickers. Pickers are a hardy lot. They can travel up to 20 kilometres a day foraging through the charred sticks of trees for the miniature sponge-like conical fungus. Their reward for such grueling work can be as much as $250 to $400 a day. They sell their load to buyers who dry them and ship them off to markets all over North America and Europe where they retail for as much as $100 a pound. I could only speculate how difficult and potentially dangerous it must be tromping in the blackened forest in the middle of nowhere for days and weeks on end.

Riding with Andy, he gave me an update since the previous afternoon. He said the elderly woman at Junction 37 had berated him, Lang and the Four Amigos for asking to pay for camping by tent rather than by person—the Mexicans had two tents between the four of them so it was cheaper that way, of course. The unfriendly woman had suggested they shouldn't be travelling if they didn't have money to pay the going rate for accommodation. Andy laughed when he described her little tirade in which she said she was fed up with cyclists wanting something for nothing. (No wonder the place was up for sale.) The convoy decided to move on and spent the night in a clearing behind the "Welcome to BC" sign a kilometre south.

Lang had left earlier than the others wanting to get a jump-start on those who were faster than him. Andy stayed with the amigos and managed to get them on the road an hour earlier than usual. I was now below the 60th parallel—a latitude that provides much of the border between BC and the Yukon—and was on the longest and loneliest stretch of road of my journey. I was glad of the company of Andy and the others. Though relative strangers and much younger than me, I felt comfortable being among them and the fact we were on similar journeys gave us an easy camaraderie.

It had been overcast all morning and had just begun to rain when the amigos, who were slightly ahead of Andy and me, suddenly stopped. They signaled to us to be quiet and pointed to the side of the road. A grizzly sow and her two cubs were feeding at the far edge of the road by the trees. I felt like I was intruding on an intimate family gathering:

heads down, the mother's humped shoulder and turned up nose revealing her kind; the three animals slowly moving and nudging one another as they grazed—utterly familiar and content with their own world. They were oblivious to our presence and our silent frenzy to reach for cameras and take shots. It was a cub that spotted us and scampered into the trees with the other following. Mother? She reared on hind legs to see what the fuss was. Noticing us she gave a long stare then dropped and sauntered after her offspring. I felt the same surge of adrenalin and hair tightening as with my black bear. It was the first grizzly sighting for all of us. Our serious, concentrated faces soon broadened into smiles as we congratulated ourselves on being so lucky.

It had stopped raining by the time we ate lunch in a clearing on the side of the road. My fruit, cheese, crackers and juice looked meager beside what the youngsters began to spread in front of them. Out came the cans of sardines, the bagels, the Nutella jars, the dried fruit. They were eating far more than I was used to consuming. I joked that they were "growing lads" and needed to load up. Andy had introduced the Nutella to the amigos when they had first met in Alaska. He thought it the ideal touring food maintaining that its composition of nuts and chocolate was the perfect combination of carbohydrates, protein and fat for endurance cycling, especially when slathered, copiously, on a raisin bagel. My own tastes ran more toward the savory—thus the cheese and crackers. I like canned fish—tuna, salmon, sardines, even oysters and mussels—but, given I had a preoccupation with keeping my load light, I only had a few cans of oysters to supplement my evening meals and was reluctant to carry more until my other food supplies started to dwindle.

My destination for the day was Boya Lake Provincial Park,

a 90-kilometre distance from Nugget City. The next possible camping spot was Jade City—a further 36 kilometres south. I'd just done two longish days back to back (125 and 114 kilometres respectively) and didn't want to push my luck, seeing how good I was feeling. Andy and the amigos were headed for Jade City where they'd meet Lang. We said goodbye as I swung left to descend the two-kilometre hill to the park.

Boya Lake Park is one of BC's most northerly provincial park campgrounds and it's situated right on the shores of the aquamarine lake. Although I'd found a beautiful spot, setting up camp was a chore solely because of the dreaded mosquitoes. Of course they'd been a constant irritant since my ride started but I'd coped quite well by smearing Muskol lotion on my exposed parts whenever I stopped for a break or to camp at the end of the day. But here, at Boya Lake, they were the worst I'd experienced so far. Not to be outdone by the swarming "mozzies," I put on my bug-proof mesh suit. With top-to-bottom protection I was able to walk, sit, eat—do whatever I liked outside—with impunity. I might look weird, I thought, but I didn't care. I'd got one over on the nasty little bug. That evening I strolled along the shoreline and watched the sun settle and hover over the nearby mountains. It was the closest I'd come to watching a sunset since I'd left home a week earlier.

DAY 6 Boya Lake Provincial Park to Dease Lake

Variously named the Stewart-Cassiar Highway, the Dease Lake Highway, the Stikine Highway or simply Highway 37, my new highway was a much narrower and lumpier road than the Alaska Highway. Its multiple names reflect the geography and landforms it travels through. Cassiar is the name of an abandoned asbestos mining town in the Cassiar Mountains some 130 kilometres south of Junction 37. The town and mountains along with the town of Stewart almost 600 kilometres to the south inspired the most popular of the highway's appellations and it's the one I chose to use most of the time. I'd been riding through the Cassiars for the past three days and would continue for a few more. The other two eponymous names for the highway derive from Dease Lake, which is both a body of water (naturally) and a small town at the lake's southern end and is situated roughly a third of the way down the highway, and the Stikine —one of BC's signature rivers noted for its dramatic canyon and as a prolific spawning ground for coho, sockeye and Chinook salmon.

I left Boya Lake with the sky bright and clear. Within the hour I was riding along the silvery blue waters of Good Hope Lake. Mount Pendleton, to the south, was sitting as a magnificent backdrop, its craggy north face a patchwork of light and shade—the snow on its pyramidal top glinting in the early morning sun. I stopped at the grocery store in the tiny community of Good Hope Lake wanting to buy a few supplies. The door was open and a mangy-looking dog lay sprawled across the entrance. It raised its head lethargically as I stepped over it into a large but sparsely stocked room. There was a freezer, and a refrigerator with some dairy products along the back wall and a few shelves of mostly snack foods. There was cheese but of the sliced variety and I gave it a miss. No one was behind the counter so I called out "hello" a couple of times. Some moments later a young woman immerged from a back room, hair disheveled and rubbing her eyes with the back of her hands. I'd spotted some packets of crackers on the counter. They had no cardboard packaging just the cellophane wrapping. (I assumed they were past the "Best by" date.) I asked their cost and paid her the toonie she'd guessed at. Outside and back in the sunlight I tried to imagine what it must be like for a youngster living surrounded by such natural grandeur. Unless they'd manage not to utterly succumb to the modern ethos, I imagined it could be a wonderfully energetic and fulfilling life. If not, I mused, a life of desperation could ensue. With the image of the drowsy young woman in my head I made my way toward Jade City and the remains of the convoy.

As I'd hoped, Andy and the amigos were waiting for me outside the small community's jade store. As I approached its entrance walkway I was greeted with loud cheering as I pedalled to a stop. Not only was the gang (This is what I called them now that the others of the convoy were no longer part of the group.) outside but also the storeowner and her young staff and a few customers. I felt very touched by the welcome and a few moments later, inside the store, when people approached me to say how impressed they were both with my ride and the fund raising I'd already accomplished. (At that time it had only been four weeks since starting my fund raising and I'd collected over $4,000.) The gang had camped in the campground beside the store and had been treated royally by the store's peppy female staff and some other youngsters who were also camping. I was immediately plied with hot apple cider (I could have had coffee or tea)—all I could drink—on the house. Sipping away, I began nattering to one of the staff and getting her suggestions as to what jewelry I might buy for Lorinda and Mia. The store, I was told by the owner, was named to recognize the Princess Jade Mine, a mine close by with the reputation of being one of the largest jade claims in the world. I was surprised to find this out, as I was by the large display of jewelry, ornaments and souvenirs the store had. In my tiny mind, I'd only associated jade with China and the trinkets and ornaments sold in the Chinatowns I'd visited in Victoria, Vancouver and San Francisco. Jade, I've since found out, has a long history in the cultures of not only China but also of India, Burma, Korea, of the New Zealand Maoris and the ancient Mayan and Olmec cultures of Guatemala. BC jade is a relative newcomer. But it might not be surprising. One of the minerals in the makeup of jade is nephrite which, in turn, has actinolite as a constituent—a form of asbestos. The ghost town of Cassiar (which I've already mentioned), a few kilometres away, once served a thriving asbestos mine (until, you know what, happened). Again, in my tiny mind, I'd say, where there's asbestos, jade might be found. Outside the store, as I looked around me, I realized that, not unlike the Quesnellia Terrane I passed two days earlier, the primordial forces of nature had wreaked havoc with the surrounding mountainous landscape and in so doing had endowed it with a profusion of minerals and ores the modern world now regards as riches.

Lang, the young Korean, as was his pattern, had left early, so it was just the six of us who set out for the day's destination of Dease Lake. The Four Amigos sped ahead while Andy was content to ride with me at a more moderate pace. The volcanic-coned mountains seemed to dominate the skyline at every turn in the road. They appeared as if perfectly shaped by some giant sculptor's chisel, their pointed summits puncturing the clear morning sky. I could hardly differentiate one peak from another so uniform were their contours.

On my way to Jade City I'd passed a large road-construction sign saying that there'd be road works for the next 84 kilometres. It seemed rather a long stretch to have ongoing road repairs but I assumed in such a harsh winter climate road surfaces would get a beating. In reality, I hadn't seen a road crew since the sign, so I was perplexed as to what the sign really meant. Just before I met the gang, the asphalt had occasionally morphed into fine grade gravel. Although dusty when vehicles passed, the surface was very rideable. By four o'clock Andy and I came upon a work crew. Graders, stream rollers, gravel trucks and other road-building machinery stretched for hundreds of metres into the dust-hazed distance. A tall, heavily-built flag lady waved us to a stop. As we came to a halt a pilot truck was turning around after leading a small convoy of cars and trucks coming from the south.

"You'll have to take the pilot truck. Your bikes can go in the back," the big woman ordered.

"We can't do that." I was speaking for myself but I assumed Andy would have said the same. "We're riding all the way through BC. We can't accept a lift."

"You got to. You'll get killed out there. Those truck drivers'll never see you in this dust."

I continued my protest but Andy interrupted and said. "John, she's right. Let's get in the truck."

With that she started talking on her walkie-talkie and called the pilot truck to come and pick us up. Taking our panniers off our bikes we loaded them into the truck's box and climbed into its spacious cab. I realized straight away, once we were moving, the flag lady was absolutely right. Looking out the cab's rear window I could see dust billowing in our wake as we threaded our way between huge equipment, gravel trucks loading and unloading their cargo and grimy looking hard-hatted work crews. Not only would Andy and I have been invisible, we'd have been covered in sand-coloured dust in no time. We'd been loaded in the truck at Canyon Creek and by the time we were getting our bikes and panniers out at Sawmill Point at the north end of Dease Lake we'd been driven 20 kilometres. No doubt about it, I was disappointed not to have ridden those 20 kilometres, but I was thankful for the safety of the lift.

The flag lady had told us the Four Amigos and Lang had been ferried by the pilot truck not long before us so we weren't surprised to come across them a few kilometres after we were dropped. They were on the side of the road in a rough clearing surrounding Lang's bike. He'd had a flat. Worse, his tire was toast. By the time Andy and I arrived Lang had already negotiated with Mario (yes, he really is Mexican despite his Italianate name) to buy his used spare. Lang was in a bit of a pickle as he'd made a bad choice of tire in Seoul. Now he was paying for it. He'd worn out the two spares he'd brought with him and, from where we were, the closest bike shop was 570 kilometres away in Terrace. (Lang and the amigos were heading for Prince Rupert to take the ferry to Port Hardy. They would then cycle down Vancouver Island to Nanaimo, catch the ferry to Vancouver and ride south from there. Terrace is on the road to Prince Rupert.) Mario's tire was fairly well worn. The rest of us had larger wheels so those who had a spare (I didn't) couldn't offer. (Alex, Pedro and Louie were riding Surly touring bikes, like Andy. I was on a MEC hybrid. Our wheel size was 700C. Mario and Lang had mountain bikes with 26-inch wheels.) We all agreed that Lang's excessive load was the likely culprit of his worn tire. When we were satisfied that Lang's bike was rideable again, we all set off for Dease Lake—about a two-hour ride away.

My companion for this short, late afternoon ride to the small town was Mario. Of the four, he'd started the least fit. As we chatted, he told me that he'd gone to New York to improve his English after he'd graduated. He'd found little work in his profession as a design engineer so had waited tables for most of the past year. He hadn't been as physically active as during his undergraduate days and was pleased with his progress so far. "You should have seen me during the first week. I was really hurting trying to keep up." He was a tallish, fine-featured man with a short beard and dark hair framing his face and settling just above his shoulders. Like his three friends, he was from a wealthy Guadalajara family. We spoke of the drugs and violence in Mexico and how discouraged he felt at their seemingly intractable grip on a society plagued by poverty and an ineffective political establishment which lacked the will to end the corruption.

We arrived in Dease Lake shortly before seven o'clock. Fortunately for us, the community's main grocery store was at the north end of town and was almost the first building we clapped eyes on. It, along with the adjacent liquor store, was about to close. During a quick survey of the store's offerings I suggested we buy a twelve pack to share among us. Everyone agreed, so Andy, Louie and I went next door and bought 12 cold Molson Canadian. Andy thought it an appropriate beer for the occasion and Louie was delighted to be introduced to a Canadian beer—until now he'd only tasted American beer. Half a block from the store was an abandoned small log house. We parked our bikes at the side of the building and made ourselves comfortable on the steps of the front porch. Though not an exceptionally long day (kilometre-wise, I'd covered 144 but 20 of those had been in the semi-hermetically-sealed truck cab), it had been hot and I knew a beer or two would be well deserved and refreshing. After downing the first can everyone relaxed and the banter among us was largely humorous as we went over the day's ride. Lang's tire incident was, as you might imagine, prime fodder. Louie, while rummaging in his portable handlebar bag, laid a copy of Immanuel Kant's philosophy on the steps. I asked if he liked Kant. He replied, "If I understood him, I might be able to answer that question." I jokingly suggested a less painful way of studying Kant was to use Wikipedia. He chuckled in agreement.

We'd all heard or read about a RV park and campground in the town so we asked a passing couple for directions. It was on the south end of town, no more than 300 metres away. I don't know what it is about elderly operators of RV parks but some are not well disposed to having bike tourists stay on their property. We walked into the park's office and rang the bell. After a longish wait (and another ring) an elderly man appeared. There was no greeting, no "And how can I help you?" just a blank stare. We asked if we could stay and what it would cost. Although there were seven of us, we only needed space for five tents. He replied that he charged by person not by tent. (The gang had heard this before!) Though the cost wasn't exorbitant, we asked if he'd reconsider. He said no. I asked if he charged his RV customers by vehicle or by persons in the vehicle, he said by vehicle. I pointed out the inconsistency in his logic. Why couldn't we, then, pay by tent? He wouldn't budge. We left the office to talk it over. Andy had been told by one of the grocery store staff of a free primitive campground half-a-kilometre south of town and suggested we go for that. Looking around, we saw an expanse of grass with some hookups but no picnic tables. Not very appealing. What was appealing, to me at least, were the showers. I said I would stay, the others decided to go down the road. When I went to pay for my site, the man was no friendlier. He'd just lost six paying customers because of his surliness and intransigence.

Was it the isolation or the long, harsh winters that made some folk seem unhappy or was it a tinge of envy or regret for a life they'd never lived? I wondered. Coincidentally, we'd all decided that Dease Lake would be a day off, so we arranged to meet the following day at the café next to the grocery store. After six days on the road, I thought it prudent not to push my luck with regard to how good I was feeling. Originally, I'd planned my first rest day at Smithers but decided 11 days on the bike without a break might be pushing it. Dease Lake was a good compromise, having a good grocery store, a café and a respectable motel. That evening I phoned Lorinda and Mia from the campground payphone. Mia was enjoying writing her facebook blog and wanted every detail, every nuance of my experiences. She was thrilled that so many people were following my trip through her words. She needed photos, she said. Perhaps I could send her some from Smithers in five days time. I said I'd try. Lorinda reacted with relief when I told her I was riding in company much of the time. Her main concern was that I wouldn't be completely alone riding the long stretches between campgrounds. I was doing just fine, I assured her.

Day 7 Dease Lake Rest Day

I woke early but decided to snooze for a while. A sleep-in would be good I told myself. It was a rest day after all. I heard my alarm go off and then the sound of rain beginning to fall. The idea of dealing with wet gear after my Teslin escapade was bordering on paranoia. I'd scoped out the shower and washroom building the night before just in case I needed shelter. There was a large overhang that would work. I was dressed and carrying my sleeping stuff and pannie shower building within moments. In the early morn I noticed a gazebo-style building behind a line of bus metres from the showers. I hadn't noticed it in the d previous night. Perfect. I'd take my gear and bike t be completely dry while I made breakfast on its lar table. As I was spreading my damp tent fly on the railing a young couple emerged from a panel truck few metres away and came to join me. I recognized from the night before; I'd shown him the combinatio the shower room door. We said our good mornings ar to chat. They were from Switzerland; their names C Raphael; they were on a world tour. Seeing I was pre with arranging my gear they invited me to share th fast. Olivia was an editor for a Swiss travel maga Raphael a filmmaker. Their English was impeccable, e his. He'd worked in central BC for a year before stud at the Vancouver Film School. They were keen hikers disappointed not to have come across many accessib trails in the northern part of the province. They w Telegraph Creek in the hope of glimpsing the Stiki canyon (sometimes referred to as the Grand Canyon kine), and to hike in Mount Edziza Provincial Park. T tain is the tallest volcano in Canada and, at 2,787 met ft), dominates the skyline for kilometres. Apparent access to the park south of Telegraph Creek but i a boat trip across the Stikine. They would try their l

I left the campground late morning and head larger of the town's two motels, the Northway In because of the rain and partly to make my rest da ful" as possible, I decided to book myself into this clean and tidy motel. Check-in time was 3 p.m. but persuaded the manager to let me in at 2. I left my bike and gear at the motel and went to buy some supplies and search for the gang. The Four Amigos had made themselves comfortable in the town's café-cum-laundromat-cum-convenience store's lounge area. They'd been there for some time keeping out of the rain. Lang had left for nobody-knew-where and Andy was about to go and hang out where he'd camped that night. Before I left for my motel room I arranged to have dinner with the Four Amigos in the café at six.

Over dinner I had a chance to get to know the four young Mexicans a little better. I've always amazed how we tend to instantly gravitate to one person in a group, especially when you first meet. Louie was the one I had an immediate rapport with. He was studying philosophy and had an interest in English literature. He was tall, sported a wispy beard and always seemed to be smiling. His given name was Luciano but preferred Louie. I ask why he and Mario had Italian names. He said it was not unusual for Mexicans parents to give Italian names to their offspring. Pedro was studying drafting and looked the most Mexican of the four (at least that's what his three friends jokingly told me). Alex was a tall, rangy man with a broad grin, which lightened his otherwise serious face. He was studying music with a speciality in composition. He had learned the piano as a child but now preferred the violin. On the bike, he was by far the most talented and would take off most days to ride out front, on his own. Except for Mario, the three had trained for the trip by riding to and fro the University of Guadalajara campus every day—a 45-minute journey each way. I asked where they'd be camping that night. A local First Nations woman had offered them her basement, so they were happy and would be kept dry. We parted with a "Might see you in the morning, then?"

farewell. Unbeknownst to any of us, that would be the last time we would see or speak to one another.

Day 8 Dease Lake to Tatogga Lake Resort

It had rained throughout the night and was still drizzling when I cycled out of the motel's courtyard. I felt well rested and was looking forward to riding on the edge of the wild expanse of the Spatsizi Plateau which is now one of BC's largest wilderness parks. Unless a miracle happened and the rain stopped and the clouds lifted I knew I was going to be disappointed and see very little. I would make the best of a bad day, weather-wise, I told myself, and just enjoy being in its sphere.

Approaching the first hill out of town I could see another work crew with its assortment of trucks and graders halfway up the slope (aptly named Broken Hill). A short queue of vehicles was stopped behind a flag lady. I rode up beside the front vehicle, a delivery van, wet mud splashed on its side. The flag lady pointed to me and shouted, " You'll have to take a pilot truck. Wait there." The reverse of two days ago was happening. Instead of clouds of yellowy dust billowing in the air, the road surface was being churned into a gravelly quagmire. After the line of traffic was lead through, the flag lady called another truck over and I was driven the bumpy two kilometres out of the work area. I didn't protest. But I felt compromised doing it. And I'll tell you why. Sitting next to the driver I began to recall a story I'd read during my trip research. In a 1973 issue of National Geographic I found an article entitled: "Bikepacking Across Alaska and Canada." It was written by Dan Burden, an early pioneer of long-distance cycling in the US. He, his wife, Lys and two friends, June and Greg Siple, set out from Anchorage, Alaska in June of 1972 to ride to their home town of Missoula, Montana over some of the roughest roads they could find. Eschewing the relatively well travelled but unpaved Alaska Highway they decided to strike out from Watson Lake down the unfinished Stewart-Cassiar Highway. One hundred and sixty kilometres south of Dease Lake they ran out of road. They were staring at a sea of mud. Here's how Burden described their encounter:

> *Mud, bicycling's old nemesis, gripped us in a stranglehold. Clogging our wheels, it slowed us to a walk on a newly bulldozed track that ripped through the wilderness like a raw wound. Now it clutched at our ankles, slopped at our knees, and pulled Greg and me to a stop in front of a wide syrupy pool. "It looks at least waist deep in there," Greg said.*
>
> *Summer downpours had softened this incomplete gap in British Columbia's Stewart-Cassiar Highway, and heavy road-making equipment churned it into a ribbon of slate-gray muck. To our left the roadway dropped into dense forest. On the right loomed a steep, slippery embankment. Perhaps the store owner at Dease Lake, a hundred miles back, had been right. "You're going to cross the gap with those?' he exclaimed, eyeing our equipment-laden 10-speeds. "Impossible!"*
>
> *A highway worker on a completed stretch of road had taken a more optimistic view. "On bikes, well... you might make it through."*

They did, of course. But what a journey it must have been. Though only in their late twenties, the four were trailblazers for the rest of us who, over the years, have covered the same distance, ridden through the same wilderness, in some of the same lousy weather and have experienced the deep satisfaction of riding the Stewart-Cassiar. I felt very wimpy perched next to the driver in the warmth and dryness of his truck. At least I had my aging body to provide a partial excuse, I told myself, as I imagined the four dragging their bodies and gear-laden bikes through the mire on that miserable day over forty years ago.

The terrain slowly changed as I rode into the late morning. The road was no longer a narrow channel through a wall of trees but a clear and wide track atop a sprawling expanse of sub-alpine tundra. I reached Gnat Pass, its summit-sign telling me I was at 1,241 metres (4,071 ft)—the highest point on the Stewart-Cassiar Highway. In the misty light I could see the stunted conifers and low shrubs so typical of the tundra. Lower Gnat Lake loomed like a mirage out of the low clouds. Occasionally I could make out the vestiges of the abandoned BC Rail railroad bed that was paralleling the road—a lesion on the landscape that can still be seen from Google Earth. As I surmised earlier, the mountains of the plateau were hidden from view but my imagination was hard at work creating pictures of what they might look like. I also consoled myself with the thought I'd be crossing the Stikine River in an hour's time.

Rolling off the summit I saw a rider slowly coming towards me. Apart from the gang, he was the first cyclist I'd seen in over a week. He wasn't a young man; his deeply-tanned craggy face and graying hair announced that fact. Despite our brief encounter, I found his story fascinating. He'd been on the road—on his bike—for over 20 years. In 1989 he'd decided to cycle, solo, around India. He enjoyed it so much he's never stopped. He'd cycled all over the world and was now on his way from San Francisco to Alaska, "just to see what it looks like," he told me. He'd made a lifestyle of his wanderlust. His bike was very heavily loaded—more so than either Lang's or Brian the Brit's. He'd bought the thing in New York in 1991 and, apart from the frame, he'd replaced every part of it numerous times. Before we parted I asked his age. "Turned 61 this year." was his reply. As I started the long descent he'd just climbed, down to the Stikine, I wondered what kind of man he was. He didn't have the air of a hobo or a homeless person—he had good cycling gear and good equipment. He was English and that made me think, "Remittance Man." In 19th century Britain, a remittance man was a male who, for whatever reason, was dispatched to a colony to live far away from the family home. Usually from a wealthy family, they were given enough money to live a respectable life abroad. Perhaps my English cyclist, I speculated, was a latter-day remittance man, using family money to support his travels. Whatever his history, he seemed to be living an adventuresome life. And, I wasn't the only "Old Codger" out there.

I caught sight of the river as I freewheeled down the long, steep grade to the Stikine Bridge. It was to my left and, finding a clearing in the trees, I stopped to get a good, long look at it. At this point in its journey it was flowing west through a wide, flat valley—a flood plain with extensive sandbars that split the river into large channels. From photographs I'd seen, I knew the mountains beyond its southern banks rose up gradually and were the front of the modestly-high Eaglenest Range to the south. In clear weather I would have seen their snow-tipped peaks. As it was I was happy just to be here. I continued down to the bridge—an unimpressive beam and girder structure that did no justice to the reputation of the waters flowing beneath it. I peered over its side to absorb as much of the now-churning river as I could, its chocolate-coloured mass gliding between the glistening rock walls that defined its course. Rain started to fall again but I was content to stand and contemplate the river as it rushed on its journey to the coast. I'd read that the American explorer, naturalist and father of the American national park system, John Muir, had in 1879 navigated the lower part of the river and was overwhelmed by its grandeur and the awe-inspiring landscape it had etched. He was so taken with its canyon he reputedly called it the "Yosemite of the North." Such was the power of the river flowing beneath me.

The road up from the bridge was steep, long, and, for the first kilometre, gravel. Each year apparently, that part of the road gets washed out by snow slides. The highways department decided it was too expensive to repeatedly repair with asphalt so have left its surface gravel. After the final 8% grade and seven kilometres from the bridge I stopped at a tourist information board with a covered roof. I would lunch here and get out of the rain. While I was eating a Subaru Forester pulled into the small parking area. A young woman got out and started to rearrange the back seating compartment which I could see, from where I was standing, was crammed with personal belongings. We nodded to each other an hello. When she had finished rearranging she walk up to me and offered me a fruit juice and an energy bar. I thanked her but declined saying I had plenty to eat. We talked briefly. She was on her way from Whitehorse to Smithers to start a new job. As she drove away, I thought how thoughtful she'd been. As with the guy at Teslin, it was another expression of the generosity of strangers.

The rest of the day's ride was rather dreary. I knew the kind of scenery I was missing but I was resigned and philosophical enough not to let it worry me. I rode along in my own world, whistling and singing to the damp and now chilly air—my thoughts in free form. One of the psychological techniques I'd learned and used as a competitive athlete was what is known as association and disassociation. One of the elements that differentiates winners from the also-ran, is the athlete's ability to associate with his or her pain. That is, to accept it, tolerate it, monitor it and push it to the limits. The winner of a race is not always the most physically gifted but the one who can suffer the most. The flip side of that is disassociation. This is when an athlete is in so much pain and discomfort they conjure up thoughts that distract them from what they are physically feeling. Sometimes these thoughts are of a difficult workout that turned out well and can be used to self-motivate to keep pushing. At other times they are pleasant thoughts, of sunshine and beaches, of being with family and friends. These thoughts are useful when a race is not going well or in a long distance event when it's difficult to stay with the discomfort every moment. Of course, this technique can be useful in many aspects of one's life. On my journey so far, after almost 700 kilometres and six full days of riding, I used both association and disassociation. The former when climbing those long 7 and 8% hills (and steeper in the days to come), and the latter on days like this one when all I could see was on the white line of the road in front of me.

I stopped at Iskut, a Talhtan First Nation village. It had a modest grocery store and what looked like a brand new housing sub-division idyllically set in a forest of spruce and pine. I was also in Wade Davis country. He's the renowned

Canadian ethnobotanist, environmentalist, writer and filmmaker—an extraordinary man—who has a home a stone's throw away on Ealua Lake. He has deep roots in the community and in the surrounding wilderness. And when he's not there he's in Washington, DC being the explorer-in-residence at the National Geographic Society. (An oxymoron if ever there was one—"explorer-in-residence!") While I was writing this book, Davis was on a tour promoting his latest book *The Sacred Headwaters* which, besides being a gorgeously illustrated work is, as its subtitle *The Fight to Save the Stikine, Skeena and Nass* clearly indicates, an argument for the preservation of an incredibly diverse and precious (and still largely intact) wilderness area. As I could see from the helicopters flying overhead with all sorts of equipment dangling from their bellies that afternoon, the mining and other extraction industries were very interested in the area. Davis's intent is to halt two mining proposals near Iskut—a gold mine and an open-pit copper operation—and to persuade Shell from pursuing shale-gas extraction and instead keep intact permanently, a moratorium on such development. Davis likens the whole area I was in and about to penetrate further to some of the world's most spectacular places like the Serengeti Desert, the Grand Canyon and Yosemite National Park. I wish him success and, quite honestly, back then, on my bike, I wished I could have seen more of that incredible landscape I hope will be protected forever.

My day's objective was Tatogga Lake Resort—a reasonable 100 kilometres from Dease Lake. I thought I might have bumped into Andy and Lang and even the Four Amigos but no, they were nowhere to be seen. Mid-afternoon the rain tapered off although the clouds still hung low over the surrounding mountains. Before I checked in at the resort's heavily-timbered lodge I rode toward the lake to look at its camping sites and to see if Andy and Lang had arrived. (I'd told them that this is where I'd stop once I left Dease Lake.) Neither of them was there nor was anyone else. Apart from two RVs, the place was deserted. Well, not quite. At the edge of the lake there was lots of activity. Behind a large cordoned-off area was a group of men standing by lengths of neatly stacked piping. A helicopter was nearby, its whirling rotary blades causing wavelets on the lake. As I turned to go up to the lodge a huge tractor-trailer came creeping down to the lake laden with god-knows-what. This was no ordinary resort I complained to myself.

The campsites were not well maintained and were set amongst mosquito-infested trees. I wasn't looking forward to spending a night there. I'd noticed a group of small cabins not far from the lodge and went to investigate. "Rustic" was how the resort's brochure described them. That was about right. The rain had started again so I decided to take one. Walking along the veranda toward the lodge's front door, a young woman came out and said, "Andy says he'll meet you out front tomorrow at nine." "How did you know the message was for me?" I asked. "He was on the phone when you were walking up. He described you perfectly." I booked the cabin (Beaver Lodge it was named. Next door was Wolf Den) and asked what the option of "dry camping" meant in their brochure. I'd never heard that term before. The woman said, "You're in one." The best thing about the cabin was its airtight wood stove which I lit right away. On its small porch was a box full of dry wood that would last until morning. At least I'd be toasty.

The lodge, I found out that evening while quizzing the owner, Teena Wright, was built in 1956 by Tommy Walker.

Walker was a guide and outfitter and had built a thriving business taking wealthy patrons into the wilds of the Spatsizi Plateau to hunt and fish. The place had clearly seen better days but Wright was determined to bring it back to its former glory. The long dining room tables had been cleared of dinner plates and were replaced with laptop computers with a half-dozen geologists and engineers pecking at their keys. The walls were hung with large antlered heads of moose and caribou. On one side of the stone fireplace was a life-sized moose, the other a howling wolf. The whole room was a taxidermist's heaven. It seemed obvious that the resort's clients were no longer hunters and fishers of game and fish but of materials that required more disruptive and disturbing guiding practices. Before returning to my cozy-warm cabin, I spent half-an-hour in a cold call box talking with Lorinda and Mia.

DAY 9 Tatogga Lake Resort to Bell II Lodge

Andy had spent the night camping at the Red Goat Lodge 20 kilometres short of Tatogga Lake Resort along with Lang and the Four Amigos. When we met outside the lodge he was munching on a sticky bun he'd bought inside. "Couldn't resist. They looked sooo good." He was smiling as usual. I was pleased to see him again. Two days earlier, on our ride together from Jade City, he'd asked if I'd ever ridden a century (a 100 miles or 160 kilometres in my language) in one day. I told him, yes, many times. He'd never done one and was anxious to try. (Riding a century is a bit of a Holy Grail in the cycling fraternity.) The previous day he'd done his homework and calculated that from Red Goat Lodge to Bell II (my destination for today) was a tad over 100 miles and contemplated, if he felt up to it, joining me and do his century. That's partly why he'd phoned and arranged to meet me this morning. He knew my day's ride was about 145 kilometres and with his 20 to meet me—voila! I was ready to leave right away but he wanted more breakfast—to make sure he'd have enough energy for the distance, if he attempted it—he said. We agreed I'd start and he'd catch me later.

I was riding along the shores of the long and skinny Kinaskan Lake when Andy caught up. The clouds were still low and heavy and, as with yesterday, prevented me from seeing the mountains rising from the lake. Most disappointing was not being able to see the volcanic cone of Mount Edziza that stands at the heart of the 230,000-hectare provincial park that bears its name. I asked Andy if he was okay riding at my pace. He said it was fine. He still was uncertain he could do the 160 kilometres in one day. I was more sure of his endurance level than he was. I assured him that after having cycled almost every day for well over a month he would have no problem. He was amused by my optimism. That led into a conversation about fitness and training—actually, Andy asked the questions and I responded. "I don't know anybody your age who's as fit as you, doing what you're doing. What's the secret?" I told him about my background as a runner. How I'd always run, right from high school through college and university. During my whole adult life there might have been a few months when I hadn't run. I'd always competed, although, apart from my school and college days, I'd been most competitive in my forties, fifties and sixties. "My health and fitness is a way of life for me," I said. I described how, as I've aged, I've had to adapt to my body's diminishing ability to perform. I no longer run or ride five or six days a week.

As I've lost muscle mass and, more importantly, VO2max (that's the body's ability to absorb and utilize oxygen), I can only train three days a week. "I'm not as fast as I used to be, but I can still go long and climb the hills okay. I make every workout count." "That's obvious" Andy interjected. "I've always made time to train and I've always eaten healthily." (I was on a roll, as you can see.) "Being fit," I continued, "allows me to lead a very active life and especially to spend weeks hiking in the mountains, which I love to do."

At the mention of mountains Andy chimed in. "I know you're familiar with Yosemite and the Sierras," he said. (He'd told me that's were he lived when we first rode together.) "They're magnificent and I can't believe I work there." He was a teacher with a non-profit outdoor education organization called NatureBridge. He took kids of all ages and from a variety of backgrounds on 3- to 5-day hiking trips into Yosemite National Park and introduced them to the natural world. "You call that teaching?" I joked. "Well, when you take a group of kids and show them Half Dome and tell them it's one of the largest pieces of exposed granite in the world. And," he went on, "when I tell them if there's not enough snowfall in the mountains there'll be drought in the valleys. When I point out different wildflowers and talk about their habitat, I'd call that teaching." It was clear he had a love of nature and of the kids he worked with. Like me, he was also using his ride to raise money. It was for Wildlink, an organization that provides funds to take underprivileged youngsters into places like Yosemite. He'd raised almost $2,000 so far.

Over a brief snack break, he brought the subject back to his century ride. "Do you really think it's no big deal?" For some reason I mentioned mitochondria and went babbling on about how, when we train, these multiply in our musculature.

He was unfamiliar with the word and its physiological significance. They are the powerhouses of the body's cells, I told him. They break down glucose so our muscles can contract—can work hard and long. They are an integral part of human performance. The more mitochondria we have in our muscles, the longer and harder they can perform. How do we get more of these little critters in our muscles? Work them hard and increase the amount of oxygen we consume while working hard. Oxygen, I explained, was what the mitochondria needed to change glucose into contractile energy. That's what Andy had been doing on this trip, and before, while training on his road bike. He was working his muscles and his lungs and in so doing, had induced his mitochondria to proliferate. And that's why, I told him, he'd have no problem doing his century. With that simplistic lecture over, we talked more about him.

He'd been born and raised in Texas, first in Houston then El Paso where he'd lived until his early twenties. After getting his sociology degree from the University of Texas at El Paso he travelled a little before settling in Yosemite to teach. A couple of years ago, he'd cycled through parts of Central America. And now, at 28, he was on a quest: to cycle, over his lifetime, from the tip of Alaska to the bottom of Argentina. The ride he was now on would give him 4,345 kilometres of the 27,358 he needed to travel.

Just before we dropped down to cross the Burrage River we came across a large black sow and her two cubs feeding on the side of the road. We were almost on top of the threesome when one of the cubs spotted us and ran into the trees. The mother immediately stood on her hind legs to see what the trouble was. Her head followed us as we rode by not more than a few metres away. Our encounter happened so swiftly and was over so quickly neither the mother bear nor us had time to really react. I asked if Andy wanted to take a photograph. He said he preferred not to so, with our necks craning to watch the mother's movements, we rode on. A few kilometres later we came across another black bear. This one was dead on the side of the road. It was a fairly fresh kill as the grass over which the creature had skidded was still flattened. It lay on its side, a large round of exposed, furless flesh on its flank, where the impact had occurred, was still moist. One of its hind legs was stiffening and reaching skyward. There were no skid marks, no blood. We assumed it had been hit by a largish truck given the size of the bear and how far it had been thrown from the road's edge.

Late in the afternoon we stopped at the Bob Quinn Lake rest area. Andy had originally planned to stay overnight here. What we found was an airstrip with a pit toilet and a couple of picnic tables. The airstrip was built in the 1960s to serve mining companies in that neck of the woods and had been operational ever since. A helicopter pad had been added for the same purpose. Now that he'd seen the place Andy had a change of mind. The fact that the rest area was right next to an airstrip and very exposed (not a place conducive to camping—airstrip one side, road the other) and, he admitted, he didn't want to be outdone by a seventy-year-old, he decided to do his century ride after all. Before we left, he wrote a note for Lang and the Four Amigos letting them know he wouldn't be camping there, with them, as they'd planned. He'd push on to Bell II—with me.

About twenty kilometres north of Bell II we passed through two avalanche-prone areas. The mountains were steep and close to the road, their snow pack visible as were the chutes the avalanches had gouged from their slopes. A tangle of rock and tree debris littered both sides of the road and you could see new asphalt had recently been laid. We were riding through the Ningunsaw Pass—a narrow gorge that fell in the shadow of the towering Mount Jancowski, a 2,729-metre (8,953-ft) peak that dominates the whole skyline. (At least that's what I'd read. Shrouded in cloud, I couldn't see it myself.)

Named after the patriarch of a well-respected BC family, the Bell-Irving River is wild and narrow and famous as a steelhead fisher's paradise. It drains into the much longer Nass River, which was another river I looked forward to crossing. It also gives its name to Bell II Lodge—a large Swiss-chalet-type cluster of buildings coddled in the Skeena Mountains. After over ten hours on the road, nine of them in the saddle, the lodge's sign was a welcomed sight as Andy and I crossed a bridge over the river and parked our bikes under the impressive eaves of the log-beamed main building. The receptionist greeted us with a smile but said there was no room anywhere in the resort for us—not a suite, nor chalet, nor dorm room, nor campsite. She was sorry. Andy and I looked at each other then looked at the woman. "I've just ridden my bike from Red Goat to here—over a hundred miles, and you don't have some place for us to camp!" Andy, I hoped, wasn't about to loose his cool. Sitting down at her desk she said, "Let me have a look at the RV section." The woman stared at her computer screen and prodded its keys a few times. Still smiling, she lifted her head, "I have one RV spot left, next to the road. Why don't you try that? It's getting late. No RVers will come at this time." What a relief.

Andy, I soon found out, was a master at setting-up camp. Quick and methodical, before pitching his tent, he lit his stove and put on a pot of water for his meal. He then erected his tent and, in an orderly way, placed his pad, sleeping bag, sandals and toiletries inside. I, although organized, took twice as long. He was finishing his meal as I began heating my two cups of water for my dehydrated vegetable lasagna.

DAY 10 Bell II Lodge to Meziadin Lake Provincial Park

Drizzle began soon after I woke. I showered, broke camp and took my bike and gear over to the lodge and left them under the wide eave that hung above its restaurant windows. Andy was already halfway through a fairly lavish buffet breakfast when I joined him. It was an "all you can eat for 16 bucks" affair so I plumped for the lox and poached egg muffins with coffee and orange juice and had my fill. We talked of yesterday's ride. He admitted that doing his century wasn't as difficult as he thought. He felt no different this morning than after any other on his trip. A couple with their two young sons were sitting at the next table. They heard our conversation and asked about our journey. We told them, of course. They were friendly and curious. Getting up to go, the guy handed us forty dollars. "That'll pay for breakfast. Be safe and have a great rest of your trip." Andy and I were uncharacteristically tongue-tied but we managed a "Thank you. And a safe journey to you." After they'd gone Andy said, beaming away, "What a great way to start the day."

Before we left we poked around the lobby. We both bought snacks and juice for the road at the gift shop. According to the lodge's brochure, the place was originally named Bell 2 Crossing when it was first built in 1979 because of its proximity to the second bridge crossing the Bell-Irving River.

Back then it was a lonely gas station with a small restaurant and a few cabins. In the late 1990s it changed hands and, with the infusion of investment money, the new owner renamed it Bell II Lodge (the Arabic numeral 2 became the Roman II.) and established it as a premier heliskiing resort. Although there were a number of tourists at the lodge, there was, like Tatogga, a preponderance of mining types billeted in its accommodations. Cycling away, we watched as a group of men climbed aboard a waiting helicopter and took off.

A friend of mine in Victoria, who had lived in northern BC for a number of years and had driven the Stewart-Cassiar many times, had quipped that the road between Dease Lake and Kitwanga was essentially a tree-lined avenue and I wouldn't miss much. How wrong could he be. But he gave the truth to Edward Abbey's contention that, "A man on foot, on horseback or on a bicycle will see more, feel more, enjoy more in one mile than the motorized tourist can in a hundred miles." The drizzle stopped soon after we left the lodge. As the clouds lifted patches of blue sky appeared. I could see the surrounding mountains; fresh snow covering their upper slopes. Andy and I rode by the roiling waters of the Bell-Irving River for kilometres and even when we left its banks we could hear its noisy chatter. With its reputation as a premier steelhead river, I was surprised to see no one on its banks casting. "Great for whitewater kayaking, I'd imagine." Andy said. "I've a few buddies who'd love this." But we saw nobody, neither angler nor kayaker.

The road, tracing the river valley, was flat and easy riding. After yesterday's long ride, today's would be a comfortable 96 kilometres. Andy was still content to ride at my speed and, as we were heading to the same destination, Meziadin Lake

Provincial Park, he saw no reason to hurry. We had both read and heard about the park—how beautiful it was and how the campsites, set close to the lake, were picturesque. The gods, however, decided we had to pay for our aesthetic pleasures. After a day of undemanding terrain, we were confronted with the steepest hill either of us had encountered so far. We were no more than 10 kilometres from Meziadin when we saw it. Freewheeling down a steepish incline to the Hanna Creek crossing I shouted to Andy, "I don't like the look of that." Beyond the bridge I could see the road curve and rise sharply. I knew we were in for a grunt, and a long one at that. Over the bridge I immediately geared down—first to my middle ring and then, as the grade steepened, shifted into the middle cog on the back. Two hundred metres later I went into my granny gear (the smallest of the three rings of my pedal crank) and moved into my largest but one cog on the back. It wasn't long before I started standing—working to stay fluid on the pedals. Andy, I could see was doing the same. Standing, sitting, we were both in and out of the saddle. "Grind it out, Crouch." My usual self-talk when I have to work hard on a hill. "That's it." Actually I wasn't grinding. I was almost spinning. For me, it's a more efficient way of climbing steep hills and easier on my quads. It was a shorter climb than I expected but its grade topped out at 10%. Stopping at the hill's brake-check area, both Andy and I were breathing hard. A truck driver came over to talk. "Pretty steep hill that. Where you headed?" We told him. "Well, you have a nice long downhill from here." Pleased by that, we set off for the park.

Riding into Meziadin Provincial Park was a treat. Gliding down its entrance road we could see the lake spreading out before us. Mountains, coloured blue in the late afternoon light, rose from its far shore. The manicured-grass campsites with gravel tent pads were plentiful and we rode around the maze of the campground making sure we chose the best spot. We found it—a flat, raised area set up from the lake with low bushes and one large tree to give privacy. It wasn't too close to the washrooms and only a stone's throw away from the campground office and water pump. I spread my damp tent and fly over the bushes to dry. The breeze coming off the lake and the sun, when it came from behind the clouds, would do that in no time. The campground had no electricity apart from a diesel generator. At the office I asked the manager why such a well-used park was not on the grid. He explained that BC Parks wouldn't foot the bill for a 120-metre-long power line—the distance from the campground to the highway. I was incredulous. BC Parks, he was inferring, preferred to use an environmentally polluting power source, i.e. diesel fuel, instead of the plentiful, relatively cheap and non-polluting hydroelectricity. To boot, the cost of driving to and from the town of Stewart, a 94-kilometre round trip, to get the fuel, was also an expense—and an added pollutant. When I protested, the manager said, "Don't talk to me about it. I'm on your side. You should tell Parks BC. There's a suggestion box outside." Before I left his office I asked if I could use the phone. He said, "Go ahead, but it'll cost five bucks a minute." It was a wireless phone. If a power line was installed the phone line would follow. Outside, I wrote my protest note and stuck it in the suggestion box. I vowed to talk with the parks department once back in Victoria. (Speaking with a BC Parks manager some months after my trip, I was told the department had concrete plans to provide electricity to the park in 2013.)

Walking back across the road to my tent Lang came speeding down the hill into the campground shouting, "John,

John." He pulled up in front me. Although he was smiling, he looked exhausted. He'd ridden almost a 150 kilometres from the Bob Quinn Lake rest area to here. Still on his bike, straddling his crossbar, he said, "Here John." He fumbled in his jacket pocket and pulled out a crumpled five-dollar bill. "This is the five-dollars I owe you for the two beer in Dease Lake." I was touched and amused at the same time. "Lang, I didn't know you hadn't paid. It's okay. I don't need it." He insisted and was still insisting when the campground manager's wife came by. I asked if Lang could share Andy and my campsite—there was plenty of room for three tents. She agreed but said he would have to pay the full 16-dollar fee because he arrived separately from the two of us. I tried to reason with her but she was adamant. Lang reluctantly held onto his five bucks when I told him he should put it towards his camp fee. The vagaries of campground logic, I thought to myself. There was no sign of the Four Amigos. Lang had left them at Bob Quinn. Andy thought they'd be sticking to their 100-kilometres-a-day routine.

Over our evening meal Lang talked of his aspirations for the future. I already knew he wanted to cycle round the world but I didn't know how long he intended to take. He was a Christian, he said, and wanted to stop in different parts of the world and help the poor, especially children. "You mean, like a missionary?" I tried to clarify. "Yes. I want to go to Africa and help there." I wasn't keen to pursue his Christian beliefs or his predilection for missionary work. Because of his limited English it was easy to switch topics. It sounded as though his journey was pretty open ended. He had a sister in Vancouver, he said, and was going to stay with her for two months before travelling south. Through his church in Seoul he had contacts in most countries he planned to visit.

Somehow he'd applied for and been given a US work visa, so working in the States wouldn't be a problem. He'd earn money to pay for his travel. This diminutive character with a heavy bike and an even heavier load sitting next to me, in the middle of nowhere, was certainly a committed guy. Even a dreamer, one might say. That's part of life, I thought, to dream, to aspire. Lucky are those whose dreams and aspirations, even one, become a reality as they'd hoped. It usually takes hard work—and determination.

Day 11 Meziadin Lake Provincial Park to Kitwanga

Not long after leaving Meziadin I came to the Nass River Bridge. I was alone—Andy and Lang were still eating breakfast when I departed. (I knew Andy would catch up. Lang I wasn't sure about.) Unlike the Stikine River, which empties into the waters of the Alaska Panhandle some 400 kilometres to the north, the Nass drains into Portland Inlet in British Columbia waters. Peering over the bridge railings at the river I knew its journey to the coast was two-thirds done. Its name in English is derived from the First Nation Tlingit word Naas, meaning "intestine." No, this is not a reference to its winding course through the Skeena Mountains but to its traditionally large fish stocks that have provided food in abundance to the peoples of the area for millennia. I first heard of the river almost forty years ago when I was living in Alert Bay, a First Nation fishing settlement off the coast of Vancouver Island. I'd hear fishermen, both native and white, talk about taking their seine boats up to the Nass River when there was a particularly big run of salmon. The names of

Dixon Entrance and Portland Inlet were also talked of. Along with Prince Rupert, they were part of commercial fishing's folklore, as were the spawning grounds of the Nass and its tributaries. All were a considerable part of BC's fisheries economy back then.

Andy had not long caught up with me when we met a Swiss father-and-son duo riding north. (Those Swiss are everywhere on this trip.) They were on heavy looking mountain bikes with front shock suspension. Like me, they only had rear panniers and were obviously travelling light (notwithstanding their bikes). They were from Lucerne and had flown to Nogales in southern Arizona—on the border with Mexico, with the intent of cycling to Anchorage along as many trails and side roads as they could find. They had started on the Arizona Trail following it to southern Utah. They then rode through Utah, Idaho and Washington before hitting Vancouver Island. Riding the length of the island they then took the ferry to Prince Rupert. Andy and I were meeting them after they'd travelled the rugged Nisga'a Highway from Terrace through New Aiyansh to Cranberry Junction where they'd camped on the side of the road. Mathieu, the father, was in his early fifties, I guessed, while his son must have been in his mid twenties. The way they looked at each other and shared the conversation, one could tell they were in tune with one another. More than father and son, they were clearly the best of friends. The pair looked tanned and fit and, from the way they described their journey, they were enjoying themselves immensely.

After a lunch stop I suggested Andy take off. It would be a long day of cycling—over 150 kilometres by my reckoning, and I didn't want to hold him back. We both confessed how much we enjoyed each other's company but he agreed he needed to stretch his legs a bit. We'd meet again that evening at Kitwanga.

I wasn't long past the Nisga'a Highway turn-off at Cranberry Junction when I came across a black bear with her two cubs. They were too busy feeding to notice me as I gingerly rode past. Ten kilometres later I startled a young male bear no more than a few metres from the road's edge. If the Swiss duo had camped around here, I thought, they were damn lucky not to have been pestered (or worse) by one of these creatures. Over the next few kilometres I encountered three more bears. With each, I blew my whistle, shouted and made myself as visible as I could. Their response seemed to be, "Okay. I know you're there. Don't bother me and I won't bother you." One deigned to leave his grazing and walk across the road in front of me. Luckily, I had my camera close and took a shot. It looked a good one. "Now," I said to myself, "I don't care if I ever see another bear again." But I did, no more than a couple of kilometres down the road.

I knew I was nearing Kitwanga when I came across a sign for Gitanyow (formally known as Kitwankool). Fifteen kilometres north of Kitwanga, it's famous for its impressive totem poles. It's also famous, at least in my mind, for its connection with Emily Carr, one of Canada's foremost painters. Carr visited the First Nation village in 1927. She'd wanted to go years earlier, in 1912, but was persuaded not to because, she had been warned, the inhabitants were extremely unfriendly. In her early explorations of First Nations' art in their coastal communities of the Johnson Strait islands and Haida Gwaii, she'd been fascinated by the artistry and religious imagery of their totem poles and masks. This artwork had inspired much of her own creative work at that time. Fifteen years later she was determined to see the Kitwankool totems—not only because of their artistic quality but because she wanted to record, in her paintings of them, an art form she was sure would soon be extinct. She was wrong, of course. Poles are still being carved, but the impact of that visit and those totems influenced and inspired her work for the rest of her life. In a letter to Eric Brown, the director of the National Gallery of Canada at the time, she wrote this of her visit:

> *I went in on a wagon with the chief & his son & was very well treated. It is an awful waggon road took 7 hours & nearly bumped the life out of me. The heat & dust were terrific there were 4 indian men (one just returning from jail). I went in for two days & got held up for 5 by a terrific storm it poured rain & hail for 4 days which made working very* difficult. *I crawled into little grave houses which were clammy cold & leaky & always in the wrong spot to get the right view. I was particularly sorry not to do some better stuff there as the poles are very lovely they are in shocking repair but the carving is so tenderly done with great expression.*

The last few kilometres from Gitanyow to Kitwanga took me less than an hour—a little faster than Carr's bumpy journey 85 years ago. By the time I was registering at the village's Cassiar RV Park I'd covered 154 kilometres—my longest day so far.

Andy had arrived sometime before me and, as I learned later, had been invited to camp beside a large group of University of Texas students who were riding from Austin to Anchorage as a fundraiser for cancer. They'd taken the best spots—clustering their tents around a large gazebo, so I chose a secluded site close to a spreading cottonwood.

I was preparing my meal when Andy rode in with a small group of the riders. As we greeted each other he excitedly told me about the students and their ride. He'd been invited to a potluck supper the community had organized to support the students and was just getting back. Over the potluck, he'd mentioned my ride and said a few wanted to meet me. "Come over to the gazebo and grab a beer," he said. " They'd love to see you." I said I'd come over after my supper and for him to save me a cold one. While listening to a young guy's story of the group's trip so far, I sat and sipped at the cool liquid, savouring it as it slid down my throat. I hadn't had a beer since Dease Lake and after such a long day in the saddle, it tasted good.

Calling their fundraising journey the Texas 4000, the students were almost at the end of their 4,500-mile (7,242-kilometre) adventure. (A tad longer than their estimated 4,000 miles.) Since the ride's inception in 2003, the students (and it's a different group every year) have raised millions of dollars. There are usually 45 riders who, before they leave Austin, are split into two groups. One group rides to Anchorage via a Pacific Coast route, the other through the Rocky Mountains. The group I encountered was on the Pacific Coast route. Although they were on new road bikes and were fully supported (they had two large vans and a trailer), they were covering 120 kilometres a day over 70 days of riding. Not bad, I thought, even if they're barely over twenty. According to their website, it's the longest charity ride in the world. (Written by a true Texan, I'd say.) Taylor was the name of the young guy I was talking to. He'd been a keen cyclist since his early teens and was regarded as one of the strongest of the group. He was of slender build—typical of an endurance athlete, and was feeling sorry for himself. Two days earlier he bumped into the side of one of the vans while riding and had injured his left knee. He'd been chosen as one of half dozen riders to do a three-hundred mile (482 kilometres) ultra-long leg that would take over 12 hours, in two days time. Now, because of his sore knee, he was a doubtful starter. I told him I used a compression sleeve on my knee to stabilize the patella. I had a spare sleeve and would be happy to give it to him. It might help. His face beamed.

Finishing my beer, Lang arrived. It was another 150 plus-kilometre day for him and it showed on his wind-burnt face. Before I left for my tent, I asked Taylor to take a photograph of Andy, Lang and me. It would be the last time I'd share a campsite with Lang and possibly with Andy. I didn't want the place or the time to go unrecorded.

Perhaps it was the long day on the road or the beer, but I had one of the best night's sleep of my trip so far, despite a twenty-first birthday party the Texan youngsters had for one of their riders. Apparently, it went on until midnight. I didn't hear a thing.

The road and the sky—south of Whitehorse.

(L.) Teslin. Drying out after the storm. (R.) Christian, the Swiss, proud of the Arctic grayling he'd caught.

(L–R) Me, Nick, Louie, Andy and Lang at Walker's Lodge.

(L.) Beating the "mozzies" at Boya Lake. (R.) The bear!

Leaving the Yukon.

On the edge of the Spatsizi Plateau Wilderness Park.

The Four Amigos, Andy and me with the super friendly staff at Jade City.

Waiting For Andy at the Tatogga Lake Resort.

Following the Bell-Irving River.

Roche de Boule Mountain, New Hazelton.

A Fort? Hardly.

The Fraser Canyon northeast of Lillooet.

Daniel and my support crew.

Lunch in Duncan with Lorinda.

Saanich Inlet from the Malahat summit.

Mia just before my ride into Victoria.

Kitwanga to Prince George (410 km)

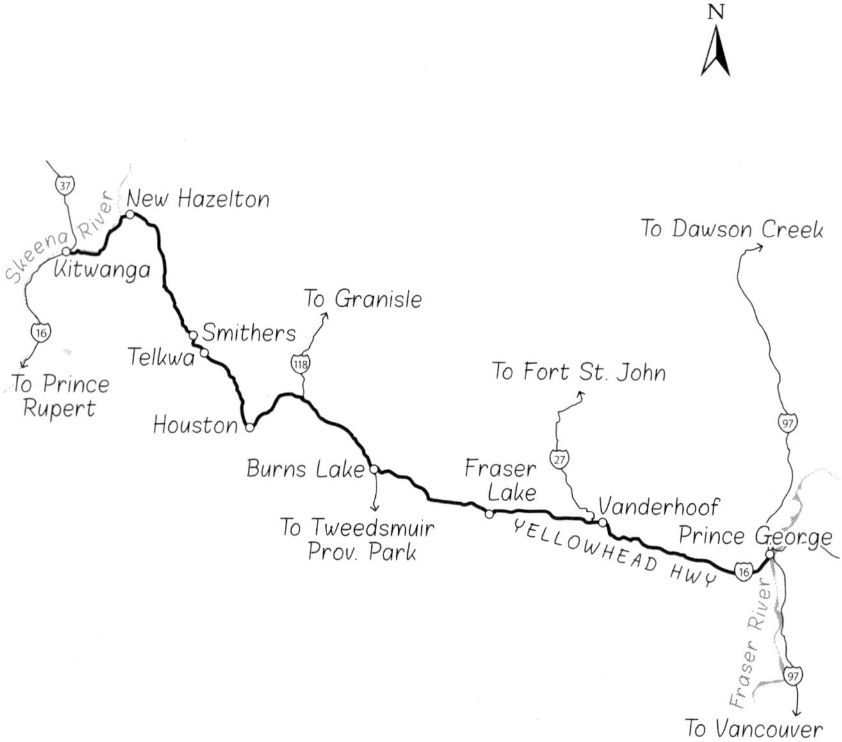

3 The Yellowhead Highway (Highway 16)
Kitwanga to Prince George

Day 12 Kitwanga to Smithers

For the first time since Teslin nine days earlier I woke to sunshine and a balmy temperature. The mountains to the southwest were brilliant as the morning sun lit their snow-covered peaks. I sat facing them as I ate breakfast, my map spread to the side. They were the Seven Sisters Peaks and I could see how they formed an imposing massif that dominated the landscape for kilometres around. They give their name to a huge provincial park that unfortunately lay in the opposite direction to my day's ride.

Andy and Lang were just starting breakfast with a group of Texans when I said goodbye. Lang gave me a big farewell hug knowing we'd likely not see each other again. This was my first deliberate leave-taking of someone I'd shared part of my journey with and we both understood the pragmatic nature of solo bike touring gives little room for sadness or regret about parting of the ways. I'd enjoyed Lang's company and he mine. We'd leave it at that. Andy, on the other hand, would catch me later in the day on the way to Smithers.

I rode toward the shining mountains and after a few kilometres turned south to cross the bridge over the Skeena River. The Skeena is BC's second longest river (the Fraser is the longest) and, like the Nass and Stikine, is a powerful and influential element in the region's First Nations peoples' culture—from what they eat to the name they bear to the wildlife that forms part of their mythology. On the bridge I stopped and contemplated the waters below. Brown with silt and swift and heavy with the waters of a myriad tributary creeks and streams, the river, I knew, provided food for both humans and wildlife. Although its commercial salmon fishery had been in decline for decades it's still a source for First Nations food fishing. While I was looking out over the river I could see a couple of First Nations fishers in a small boat trolling to and fro. It seemed appropriate that these two guys would be there, doing what their people had been doing for eons. They were the Gitxsan. Their name: "people of the Skeena River."

I'd read that the Kermode bear is native to this area and wondered if I'd clap eyes on one. (Seeing that I'd had a glut of bear sightings the previous day I thought I might be in luck.) But that wasn't likely for a number of reasons, principally because they're very few in number (between 400–1,000), they're shy and I would be out of their range later that day. Fascinating creatures though. They're a black bear with a recessive gene that gives them their white colour. They're also very efficient fishers—more so than their black cousins. That's because their white colour makes them less visible to the fish while fishing. The bear is also known by two other names—the Spirit bear and the Ghost bear. The first attest to their place in First Nations spiritual life—they never hunt them nor reveal their whereabouts to white hunters. The second describes their appearance through the mist and fog of the mountains and the inlets of the coast.

Within fifteen minutes of leaving the bridge I turned left at the junction of Highway 37 and headed east on my new highway, Highway 16 also known as the Yellowhead, named after a blond-haired Iroquois-Métis named Tête Jaune. In the early 1800s as a Hudsons's Bay Company trader, Tête Jaune was the first to push a pass through the Rockies to Prince George.

I was feeling strong and, after my good night's sleep, well rested. My day's destination was Smithers—a town of little over 5,000 set on the banks of the Bulkley River, where I would be staying with an old acquaintance, Jackie, who I hadn't seen for a dozen years or more. Jackie was a close friend of a friend of mine in Victoria and had readily agreed to play host. I was looking forward to seeing her again (along with her husband Steve and her 12-year old son Jorgen) and to spending the following day as my rest day poking about the town. I'd also do a little supply shopping and get my bike tuned-up—not that it was giving me trouble, I just wanted to keep it running smoothly. A precautionary measure, you might say.

Andy caught me about fifteen kilometres into my ride. I'd stopped to take a photograph of what looked like an abandoned church on thc cdge of the First Nation village of Kitseguecla. I was curious about its structure although it was not unlike many I'd seen throughout rural BC especially on First Nations' lands. We both rode down an approach road to the village to get a closer look at the church. Although the building looked worse for wear with peeling paint and bits of siding coming adrift it was clearly in use. Straddling our bikes as we both took photographs a villager came towards us. He was raising his voice at us although at first I couldn't make out what he was saying. He stopped in front of us and, looking at me, told me I was trespassing and that the plight of the villagers was because people like me had taken everything worthwhile and left nothing but the church. His language was foul and blunt. Before he walked on, he looked at Andy and said, "You'd know what I'm talking about. You went through that centuries ago. I'm glad the fuckers are gone. They've caused enough trouble." (We assumed he was alluding to Andy's dark skin colour and presumed his indigenous heritage.)

Soon after we rode back to the highway Andy decided to go ahead. He was making for Smithers also (to stay with a friend named Heidi). We'd look out for each other there. I was still riding at my steady pace (between 15 to 18 kilometres an hour) and making frequent stops to take photographs of the Skeena and the mountainous backdrop. I was clearly "photo" deprived after days of rain and cloud-covered skies. Nearing the small town of New Hazelton I lost sight of the river. Its replacement was the massive 914-metre (3,000-ft) dome of Roche de Boule Mountain. Its mute presence dwarfing all that surrounds it and, like most mountains, it reminded me of my own smallness. I lunched on a park bench in New Hazelton's compact downtown staring at the mountain seemingly only a short distance away. It towered over the town. There were vestiges of last winter's snow high on its northern slopes and I imagined its steep gullies turning into treacherous avalanche chutes in late winter. I looked up and over some of the town's gabled rooftops then closed my eyes. The warmth and brightness of the early afternoon sun took me into a fleeting reverie. I felt as though I was a world away sitting outside some small café in a village square in the heart of the Swiss Alps marvelling at the jagged landscape. I thought of Adrian and Christian and their home a few kilometres from the Bernese Alps and how this must have been a familiar scene for them in their home country.

The pleasant thoughts over lunch were soon overshadowed an hour later by a billboard on the side of the road. I had stopped beside a row of mailboxes at Moricetown, a village in the middle of nowhere. The billboard was directly across the road from where I'd stopped. It read: "Girls Don't Hitchhike on the Highway of Tears. Killer on the Loose." In the middle was the highway's number 16 set in a large tear surrounded by smaller tears. At the bottom of the billboard were the names and photographs of three young women beside the word "Victims." I had seen a less graphic board at the junction of Highway 37 and 16 earlier in the morning but this one was more poignant and imperative. Starting in the late 1960s until 2005 there had been an official count of 18 women who had been murdered or reported missing along the highways of central BC. Many of them were First Nations and many along Highway 16. According to First Nations' leaders, that number could be well over 40. The summer following my journey the RCMP, after many years of fruitless investigation, announced that they had matched the DNA found on one of the victims with Bobby Jack Fowler, an American rapist and murderer who had died in an Oregon state prison in 2006. The police speculated that Fowler could have been responsible for the death of nine other of the reported 18 murdered or missing women.

I pedalled on thinking of the dead women, deliberately refusing to imagine the circumstances of their deaths; and of their mourning families and how their lives would never be the same. As my mind settled back onto my day's ride I began to muse about my own experience with hitchhiking and how totally different it was. Hitchhiking was an intrinsic part of my youth and early manhood. It was how I, and many of my generation, male and female, travelled around England and across Europe. It was an accepted and exciting mode of travel and a way of adding even more adventure to already adventurous escapades. No one talked of danger or of irresponsibility. Those drivers, both men and women, who stopped and offered lifts were usually interesting people with a genuine interest in who you were and where you were going. I never once felt menaced or unsafe. Now, few would think of hitching a lift unless in a dire emergency. Not many youngsters would contemplate the act without the thought they might be imperilling themselves. But the practice still lingers especially in remote parts of the country where public transport is meager or non-existent. Youngsters continue to face the dangers associated with hitchhiking, willingly or not. It's not just the hubris of youth, or the defying of the odds but the force of necessity that makes some still persist. Clearly, we've created a society where our modern roads are not safe—in more ways than one.

It was early afternoon when I saw Andy again. No, I hadn't caught up to him. He was in a car going in the opposite direction. His friend Heidi was on her way to the Kispiox Music Festival for the weekend. They had run into each other a few kilometres away (she'd been on the lookout for him). She invited him to the festival with her—an invitation, he told me, he didn't want to refuse. As they saw me approaching, Heidi sounded her horn and stopped. They both ran across the road and Andy excitedly told me of his meeting with Heidi and about his weekend side trip. Heidi was a fresh-faced woman about Andy's age, her auburn hair in a braided ponytail. She's been living in Smithers for sometime and was meeting friends in Kispiox—a small town a dozen kilometres north of New Hazelton. It seemed doubtful Andy and I would see each other again so we said our farewells. We had swapped telephone numbers and email addresses so this might not be the ultimate goodbye. I watched them drive away, Andy's bike dangling out the hatchback door.

The topography of the area was now flatter. Mountains gave way to rolling hills. Forest morphed into farmland. I was riding through the Bulkley Valley. The day's sunshine was deteriorating into weather I'd grown accustomed to over the past week—overcast with a hint of rain. Nearing Smithers the mountains closed in again. Through the mist I could just make out Hudson Bay Mountain, an unmistakable, 2,331-metre (7,671-ft) peak rising to the south of me. Spilling from its heights a glacier played peek-a-boo in the low, swirling clouds as I tried to capture its crevasse-ridden form with my camera. Later, Jackie would tell me the mountain's backside was the local ski hill and that the glacier drains via Twin Falls into Kathlyn Lake, the area's popular swimming hole.

I'd phoned Jackie from Kitwanga letting her know I was on schedule for my planned stay. She gave me directions to her home (not too far from the highway) and I told her I'd be there between 5 and 6 p.m. On the outskirts of town I stopped and picked up a bottle of wine and half-a-dozen beer in anticipation of the fine hospitality I was about to receive. I arrived on Jackie, Steve and Jorgen's doorstep bang-on 6:30.

Jackie was much as I remembered her—a tall woman of Dutch parentage with an air of no-nonsense practicality. Steve, her husband, on the other hand, had changed considerably. He'd ballooned into a 300-pound giant. I recalled him as a muscular guy, fit from tromping about in the woods of BC as a forester. In a dozen years or so, that muscle had turned to fat. Over a nourishing meal of halibut, rice and veggies we caught up on a few of the main features of our lives since we last saw each other in Victoria. Jorgen was the big difference in family affairs. He'd just turned 12 and was the pride of his parents—naturally. He was a tall lad with a shock of straight blond hair cut to stay out of his eyes. He ate dinner quickly and went off to play with a friend he'd invited over. Steve hadn't eaten the meal Jackie, Jorgen and I had eaten. Instead, he ate pieces of very lean chicken breast. He'd just started that day on a pure protein diet in an attempt to lose some of the weight he'd gained over the years. He told me that since getting a desk job he'd let himself go. (I could see that by how he laboured up a set of stairs into the kitchen.) At 45 he needed to get in better shape. Apparently, a relative had used the diet to lose many pounds over a short period of time. Whether it was pure coincidence or the fact of my visit (and by extension my present journey and fitness level) that had prompted this moment in Steve's life to embark on such an eating regime, I'll probably never know.

I've always been aware that unfit and/or overweight people, when they meet me, are often inclined to tell me how they are just about to start a fitness and/or eating regime. They are determined to lose weight and get "in shape" they tell me. I encourage them in that pursuit and suggest that being fit and eating well are lifelong habits. They're not lifestyle fads. They take willpower, determination, organization and almost a sense of passion for them to be, over time, ingrained in who we are and how we perceive ourselves. I sometimes go on by saying it is now well understood that, no matter what we eat, be it carbohydrate, protein or fat, if it doesn't get converted into energy and then used in physical activity or as fuel for our trillions of cells, it automatically gets stored as fat. It's the complete opposite of the advice we get about using our muscles or brain. "Use it or lose it," we're told. With food it's, "If you don't use it, you keep it—as fat!"

Day 13 Rest Day

The next morning Jackie took me for a tour of the town. It was Sunday and the place seemed deserted. Back in 1913 Smithers was a railroad town being the headquarters of the Grand Trunk Pacific Railway. "Grand" is definitely not the adjective to describe the railway station that now sits on the edge of downtown and is used as a community service centre. Some years ago the town council decided to give the town an alpine theme. (A move I assume in support of the area's numerous ski resorts and a nod to its early Swiss immigrants.) Mock chalet architecture is the required style for businesses in the downtown core. At the head of Main Street there's a large fiberglass effigy of a costumed man blowing an alpenhorn. Style is easy to come by; authenticity is not. And that's what I found missing in an otherwise leafy and floral-decorated town centre. The town's only bike store was closed for the day so my hope of a bike tune-up was gone. I was giving my chain and gears almost daily oiling and although there was some slight grinding on the occasional gear shift, nothing was amiss. Prince George was only a few days away; I was sure to find a mechanic there.

That afternoon Steve downloaded my photographs from my camera onto his computer and emailed a few to Mia as I'd promised her I'd do if I got the chance at Jackie and Steve's. There were some decent shots of both the grizzly (which Steve verified as such) and her cubs and of the black bear strolling across the road. The selection I chose gave a good taste of my journey so far. Later that evening when I called, she'd already posted the bear pictures on her Facebook blog.

DAY 14 Smithers to Burns Lake

Jackie and Jorgen rode with me to the outskirts of town the following morning. They took me via the scenic route that ran along the banks of the Bulkley River. The town was obviously built on the river's flood plain and every so often there was flooding. Nothing too serious, Jackie assured me. Before we parted Jackie mentioned Hungry Hill—a long and difficult climb about 40 kilometres away. An unmistakable landmark I wouldn't miss, she said with a wry smile. I'd had a relaxing visit with Jackie, Steve and Jorgen and had a chance to relate to Jackie in a way I'd not done before. When we parted I hoped it wouldn't be the last time we saw each other.

The sky was overcast and there was a chill in the air. The first settlement I rode through was Telkwa, a tidy village hung on the southwest bank of the Bulkley River. Originally a Wet'suwet'en First Nation village but now a mixed community, it was clearly proud of itself. Its riverside park decorated with blooming flowerbeds and kempt lawn and gazebo tempted me to stop but I was intent on besting the dreaded hill before having lunch in Houston. I sighted the hill well before my tires rolled passed its large "Chain Up Area" sign—an unofficial starting line for the four-kilometre-long climb. At an average 8% grade it stretched bench-like into the distance. I grunted my way up trying to keep a steady rhythm and didn't stop until I reach the rest area at the hill's crest. I was hoping for a plaque or display revealing why and how the hill got its name. There was a display but not the one I was expecting. Below the title "The Phantom of Hungry Hill" the display was of photographs and an account of a giant grizzly that had terrorized the local livestock a dozen years earlier. It had killed several large cows and took ranchers and conservation officers three years and the killing of two other bears before it was finally felled. It weighed a massive 1012 pounds.

Rolling off the hill's 6% incline gave me a nice boost for the remaining 25 kilometres to Houston. As the bear story indicated I was back into ranch country and I could see for kilometres around. Still curious about the hill's name, I would have to wait a little longer for an explanation.

Houston has an imposing visitor centre at the west end of town. It's opposite a large grocery store where I bought some juice and then settled at a picnic table in a small park by the visitor centre to eat lunch. I noticed a couple standing next to a low building a few metres away. As I continued eating a woman and a young girl came to stand near the couple. No one had heavy luggage just small backpacks and tote bags. I imagined they were waiting for a bus. Suddenly, I heard the sound of a train approaching. It seemed to be coming out of nowhere. I hadn't noticed the tracks nearby concealed in long grass, nor that the building the small group was standing by was, in fact, a train station. (It certainly didn't look like one nor was there any signage indicating it was such.) It was the Prince George to Prince Rupert Canadian National Via Rail, five-car, passenger train. As it stopped a suited conductor stepped down from the second car and placed a stepping stool on the ground (there was no platform). The waiting group, which had now swelled to six, moved toward the conductor with tickets in hand. I watched as they boarded the train and then the conductor, looking around as if to see if there might be others wanting to get on, blew his whistle and waved his flag. The idling train slowly moved, its diesel engine noisily responding to the driver's opening the throttle. I was surprised by how intrigued I was by the affair—trains, engines, passengers, conductors—they seemed rather novel in an age were the automobile and airplane rule. But what a great way to cross the province—safe and scenic.

Finishing my lunch, I walked to the visitor centre hoping to find the answer to my question about Hungry Hill. Neither of the centre's two employees knew how the hill got its name but, as I turned to leave, a man who had overheard my question, told me he'd read the hill's name derived from the days when goods were transported west by horse-drawn wagons. The hill was so steep that the horses were usually exhausted and very hungry by the time they reached the top. A plausible enough explanation. I was satisfied.

Late afternoon I passed through Topley, a small community 30 kilometres east of Houston. Rounding a bend I met another chain up area sign. This one for Six Mile Hill. "My God," I thought, "why didn't Jackie mention this one? A ten-kilometre hill has got to be tougher than Hungry Hill." Luckily, the curving 8% grade lasted only two kilometres but it was a steep one reaching a height of 840 metres (2,756 ft) at its summit.

I realized when I looked at my computer that the hill's name referred to its distance from Topley not to its length.

The scenery remained expansive with mountains in the distance and forest and range country either side of the road. Though logging is ubiquitous throughout the area I was travelling in, on the road to Burns Lake (my day's destination) I started to become aware of large areas of clear-cut. I also noticed vast stretches of dead trees—victims of mountain pine beetle infestation. These two observations had sinister implications—as I'll explain later. Nearing the town the road ran along the shore of Decker Lake. Off to my right I noticed a bald eagle making circles over the water, fishing I presumed, for its supper. It spotted me and flew in my direction. With a swoop it dropped several metres to hover over me. It was the closest I'd ever been to such an impressive bird—I felt as though I could stretch up and touch it. What was it going to do? Dive and attack? Or was it just curious? I stopped and searched for my camera. By the time I was taking my shot, the bird was wheeling away moving in an upward gyre back over the lake. I took its brief visit as a welcoming gesture—and a propitious sign, perhaps.

I entered Burns Lake knowing I wasn't prepared to scout too long for a campground. I hadn't found anything on the Internet except a KOA campground a few kilometres east of town so the likelihood of one in town was low. It had been a long day—a kilometre shy of 150—and it was getting late. I'd noticed a motel on the left at the edge of town, its sign advertising a 10% discount for seniors. Okay, I thought, I'll ride through town and if I don't see anything I'll return to the motel. I didn't find a campground and the only other motel I could find had logging trucks in front and guys smoking and drinking on its balconies. Not an appealing place to stay.

I rode back to the motel I'd spotted. A pleasant woman signed me in and just as I was paying the phone rang. It was someone wanting a room. "I'm sorry," she spoke into the phone," but I've just let my last room." That would be to me.

So, that was what was so propitious about my eagle visitation.

DAY 15 Burns Lake to Vanderhoof

A large sign caught my eye as I rode out of town the following morning. It declared Burns Lake as the "Gateway to Tweedsmuir Park." I was surprised by this geographic reference—I'd never associated the park and the town with each other. Looking at my map I saw that the northern reaches of BC's largest provincial park were about 60 to 70 kilometres due south of the town. Although I thought it a stretch, it made sense the town would advertise itself as a portal to the park albeit after crossing Francois and Ootsa lakes, two of the province's largest bodies of water. Like many of the communities in rural BC, the town was keen to take any advantage it could find to enhance its relationship with outdoor pursuits and tourism. The name Tweedsmuir immediately tweaked resonances from my past and brought back vivid images of a solo bike tour I'd done 13 years earlier. I thought it rather synchronistic as I pedalled up the long, Holy Cross Hill out of Burns Lake with the Endako River not far away that I was recalling another hill I had negotiated (downward, thank God) by the name of Heckman Pass, in Tweedsmuir Provincial Park. That hill was 30-kilometres long and topped out at 18%. I'll never forget my plunge into the Young Creek Canyon, the gravel road clutching its walls—

the scenery stunning, the adrenalin high, the thoughts of grizzly bears feeding on ripe salmon in the river below exciting but scary.

Later that morning I saw another "tourism" sign. This one proclaiming I was in "The Lakes District." For an Englishman like myself the "s" at the end of "lake" was an important addition separating, as it does, itself from that beautiful and famous part of England, the Lake District. The English version is many times smaller than the one I was riding through with its 300 lakes (one of which—Babine Lake—stretched for 177 kilometres) and mountain ranges that are much higher than anything in England. But the English Lake District has its William Wordsworth and, for a short time, Samuel Taylor Coleridge, both of whom were inspired by living there to write some of their finest poetry. And it was where, as a young lad of 14, I was first infected with the love of hiking in hills and mountains and being "away from it all." It was my schoolteacher and his wife who took me and a small group of boys for a week's worth of hiking and youth hostelling in the area. Starting and finishing in the quintessential Lakeland town of Grasmere we stayed at a different hostel every night. We learnt map reading, trail finding and to use a compass. The heights of Great Gable and Helvellyn greeted us with views that took my breath away. Ever since that June week so many years ago, I've never tired of feasting my eyes on the natural world and its landscapes or of allowing it to embrace and nourish me in a way few things can.

I was now on my way to Vanderhoof along a stretch of the Yellowhead that continued to run through wide expanses of ranch and farmland and great swaths of spruce and pine forest. Among the grasses on the roadside I noticed for the first time the low-growing vetch and the demurely colourful

Indian paintbrush. I realized, after studying my map more carefully, I was riding on a vast plateau—the Interior Plateau, that I would follow until I reached the Coast Mountains. Its rolling, undulating landscape had, over the past two days, reminded me of the prairies—with trees replacing the grass and the horizon far far away. Though not without some significant high points, this flatland allowed me a perspective that I'd not had since my first days on the road in the Yukon. It seemed I could see for kilometres on end.

By mid-morning I'd reached a rest area where I was up close to the now endemic dead or dying conifers. Journalist Patrick White, in his cogent 2007 Walrus magazine article on the devastation the mountain pine beetle has caused in BC's forests, described this diseased timber as "bugwood." According to White, the bug had killed $50 billion worth of trees in less than ten years. The ravaging hasn't stopped, so by now the price tag must be much higher. The root cause for the infestation is climate change. Since the late 1980s the winter weather in north-central BC hasn't been cold enough to kill the pest. The conditions needed to kill it and thus retard its spread is a temperature of -40° Celsius before November or -20° Celsius or lower for two weeks or longer during the winter. The last time that happened, apparently, in this neck of the woods was in 1985.

White's article was titled "Red Rush," a play on "Gold Rush" and a nod to the russet colour of the dead and dying trees crowding the landscape. Even though the timber is dead it can be useful for up to ten years as long as it's harvested. In 2007 the rush was on to get as much useable timber (and therefore as much money) out of the catastrophe as possible. White was writing about that process—what it was doing to the communities in the region, how it was affecting local economies and what were some of the long-term effects of the changing forest (or lack of one). Even as I was travelling through the region four years after White had written his piece, my sense was that the "Rush" was still on—but was about to have unforeseen consequences. I could still see the large clear-cuts by the highway and off in the distance—brown earth and the rust colour of the woody detritus left by the loggers. During my daylong journey I passed one sawmill that was surrounded by giant bundles of dead wood, long and spindly, waiting to be fed into the mill and cut into lumber. They looked like stacks of enormous matchsticks. Clouds of dust from the mill itself hung in the air, its musty smell filling my nostrils. I couldn't help thinking how volatile it must be in places where it accumulated. I imagined the mill workers wearing masks all day long.

While I was ride my way through this devastation, the author and investigative journalist Andrew Nikiforuk was publishing his book *Empire of the Beetle,* in which he exposes the incontrovertible connection between global warming, the mountain pine beetle's march through North America's coniferous forests and man's culpability in the mess. No other of earth's creatures, other than we humans, can change a landscape as swiftly as this little insect, writes Nikiforuk. The size of a grain of rice, the beetles have killed more than 30 billion trees across the continent and it threatens to destroy the whole of Canada's boreal forest. He likens the epidemic to hurricanes—once they've started they're unstoppable. Not a happy picture.

The January following my trip, the Babine Forest Product's sawmill in Burns Lake exploded and burned to the ground killing two workers and injuring 20 others. It was a tragedy directly related to the accumulation of dust—dead-trees-being-milled dust. Four months later, a mill in Prince George exploded for the same reason. Two more workers were killed and twenty-two others injured.

I stopped for lunch in Fraser Lake, a community sitting at the head of a long lake with the same name that proudly regards itself as "The White Swan Capital of the World." The claim was on a large and colourful display board outside the visitor centre on the east side of town. The birds are migratory Trumpeter Swans—the largest of North America's waterfowl and the world's largest swan. They use the lake and neighbouring Francois Lake as a temporary home on their way to and from breeding grounds in Northern BC and Alaska. A young couple rode up to look at the board. We nodded hello. This rather laconic pair eventually told me they were from Eureka in northern Montana and were cycling to Prince Rupert and returning home via Vancouver Island and Washington State. The woman told me of a good campground in Vanderhoof. It was cheap and had great showers with lots of hot water, she said.

Of the many contrasts I'd been noting as I rode through the hinterland of the province—mountains, lakes, wide valleys, narrow gorges, forest, range, rivers, creeks, bears—the one that I was now aware of, as I cycled further south, was the increased number of small communities and homesteads I passed and how sharply they differed from one another. Small towns, like Fraser Lake, looked tidy, kempt and fairly prosperous. Fraser Lake had obviously found its "hook" as far as tourists were concerned with its emphasis on the Trumpeter Swan. Telkwa uses its river frontage as an attraction. Others appeared down on their luck—the result, I presumed, of changing economic fortunes. Burns Lake was such a place. Half its downtown was shuttered and up for sale. Endako, a tiny village west of Fraser Lake, looked terribly rundown. Not even a nearby molybdenum mine seemed to transfer any prosperity to the place.

Roadside homes and those I could see in the distance followed a similar disparity. Some looked forlorn—paint peeling, roof patched, windows hung with dingy drapes, yards strewn with abandoned vehicles and plastic play equipment and toys. Of a different hue were homes of owners who clearly cared how they looked. Whether chalet-style, modern design or a modified box construction all, more or less, were a complement to the landscape rather than a blight. There were larger homes, often set on a rising south facing slope well back from the road. I assumed they belonged to ranchers with their expansive lawns front and back and an oft-obligatory Canadian flag fluttering from a tall pole. They would not have looked out of place in an upscale enclave of any of the country's cities.

For the first time since starting my journey I began to experience lactic acid buildup in my leg muscles when I resumed pedalling after a stop. The burning sensation didn't last more than a few minutes. I hoped this wasn't the beginning of a more permanent state. I'd become familiar with the phenomenon years ago after running intervals on the track and especially after a marathon when the lactate seemed to take days to dissipate. On the bike, it rarely occurred and when it did it was reabsorbed quickly into the blood system. This day's recurrences were unusual and I couldn't think why it was happening. I'd climbed no really sleep hills. I was keeping myself hydrated, so I thought. Perhaps it was my body's way of telling me I was doing too much. I hadn't been on the bike for so many consecutive days in ages. Was this it? Was the rest of my journey going to be a painful slog?

As I rode on the sensation went away and, thankfully, rarely bothered me again.

Vanderhoof claimed for itself the "Geographic Centre of British Columbia" on a large welcome sign as I entered the town from the west. With a following wind I'd made good time from Burns Lake covering the 132 kilometres in seven hours. I had no trouble finding the town's campground on the banks of the Nechako River about a kilometre north of town. Pitching my tent in a secluded site, I felt a spasm of excitement about spending the night in its confined space, my head close to the ground and full of the scent of the hedgerow and trees metres away from my front door. In my small tent I needed to arrange my gear neatly. By habit, I always slept on the left with my panniers lying, in a row, on the right. My headlamp, journal, pen and book were in handy wall pockets close to my pillow (which was, in fact, my down jacket stuffed into a miniature pillowcase). At night I kept my watch, water bottle and wallet inches away from my head. Knowing where my belongs were gave me a simple but necessary sense of security.

After a hot shower (yes, the Montana woman was right, the water was hot and plentiful) and before I crawled into my comfy space I headed for the hotel and restaurant I'd passed about half a kilometre away to make my phone calls and eat the largest non-meat dish on the menu—I was famished.

By now my every-other-day phone call to Lorinda and Mia were routine. Of course, they were just as curious and enthusiastic about my journey as ever. Lorinda was always happiest when she knew I was spending the night in a motel. For her, as she's gotten older, the thought of camping is fraught with too many uncertainties. Would it be safe? Would I be comfortable? What about wild animals? Although we still do a bit of car-camping together, it isn't her favourite thing to do. Her imagination, I'd tease her, was too fertile. I assured her the campground I was staying at was clean (another of her concerns) and there were others camping nearby and I felt perfectly safe.

Before walking back to my campsite I phoned Mike Calloway in Prince George letting him know I was on schedule and I'd be in his hometown mid-afternoon the next day. Mike and his wife, Valerie had offered (through the Parkinson Society of BC) room and board for my stay in Prince George. I arranged to meet Mike on the outskirts of town at a prominent garden centre, a place, he said, I couldn't miss. I'd be there at 3 p.m. I told him.

Day 16 Vanderhoof to Prince George

Betty Hum at Parkinson Society British Columbia's Vancouver office had been busy. Not only had she facilitated my Prince George accommodation she'd lined up a series of media interviews that I was to give as I made my way south. The first was by phone from Vanderhoof with a journalist named Rebecca. I hadn't a clue who she was or who she worked for but Betty had arranged, via Mia, for me to phone her at 8.20 a.m. before I left town. Rebecca was a delight. Sounding young and enthusiastic she peppered me with questions about my trip. Why would an old guy like me, she asked, want to cycle the length of the province? How was it possible? What was my connection with Parkinson's? What were some of the highlights so far? She thought it "neat" that I saw so many bears and couldn't imagine cycling over a 100 kilometres in one day. I hoped she'd got all she needed for her story I told her. Yes, she said. She thought my story would appeal to many of her readers. As I left the hotel lobby where I'd made the call, I noticed a sign above the lintel. "Breakfast at 6" it read. For some, I thought, the day's almost half over.

After two weeks in the saddle I was still aware of the importance of pacing myself throughout the day. This day, like so many others, had started with a long slog uphill out of town. I reminded myself not to work too hard and let the terrain dictate my effort and pace. So far, I was successful in not letting the hills be daunting. Being on the plateau meant the hills tended to be long and steady rather than fiercely short and steep.

From my map I could see the road had started to track southeast. God knows why, I thought, as it has to veer north to enter Prince George. Ah, the mysteries of road construction. As a cyclist, sometimes you wish the road was more direct. That's not to imply I wasn't still enjoying myself—I was.

By lunchtime I found myself eating by an abandoned resort. It was the beleaguered Bednesti Lake Resort, an historic enterprise whose fortune had fluctuated for almost 80 years. Set back from the road was an impressive log structure that clearly was only a few years old. It had large hand-carved doors and I could see through the windows carved decorative support beams. It was described as an art gallery and cultural exchange centre intended to feature the art and craft of the Saik'uz First Nation who had bought the resort in 2004. I don't know what happened to close the place—the financial crash of 2008 perhaps, but it seemed a pity and I'm sure a lot of money was lost.

I'd made good time to the outskirts of Prince George and my rendezvous spot with Mike. It wasn't a sunny afternoon but the air was warm. Waiting the half hour for Mike to show passed quickly. Over the phone the previous evening he'd described his vehicle—a blue Kia minivan. He needn't have bothered. Pulling up next to my bike he jumped out and immediately shook my hand and gave me a big hug. For someone whose day's task was to meet and greet an endurance cyclist, he couldn't have been dressed more appropriately. He wore a black French beret (which complemented his white goatee perfectly), a yellow Tour de France T-shirt and black shorts. What a guy, I thought, this man knows a thing or two about cycling, or at least gives that impression. He suggested he drive ahead of me with his emergency flashers on. (We were about 8 kilometres out of Prince George.) Given the amount of traffic on the road I was not ready to incite the displeasure of drivers who might be stuck behind a 20-kilometre-an-hour minivan escorting a pannier-laden cyclist into a busy city—besides, they all seemed to be driving huge pickup trucks. I suggested instead that he meet me at the next major intersection from where we'd turn left and he'd escort me to his home. He agreed.

I whizzed down the long hill into the outskirts of town and was at the intersection in no time. I stopped at the side of the road just before the traffic lights expecting to see Mike. He wasn't there. I waited a few minutes and then decided I'd misunderstood and he'd be waiting on the side of the road after I'd made the left-hand turn. So I crossed the multi-laned intersection onto the road going to my left. No Mike. Perhaps he was a little further on where it would be easier to park on the side of the road. No. Still no sign of my host. I again waited for a while in the hope he'd show up. What happened over the next hour or so might have been right out of a TV comedy skit.

I was now on a busy divided highway. Being reluctant to retrace my route back to the intersection in case we should miss each other I continued on in the hope Mike would catch up with me. After about 15 minutes of riding I came to an overpass and what looked like a complicated junction. "That's it," I told myself. "Get off the road and make a call to Mike's home." I appeared to be on the edge of an industrial area with a couple of storefronts. I parked my bike outside one of them—a thrift store, and went in clutching my journal with Mike's phone number in it. The friendly woman behind the counter let me use her phone. A woman answered. It was Mike's wife Val. I told her what had happened and asked if she could give me her and Mike's address. We finished our brief conversation with her telling me it was typical of Mike to have predicaments like this. I left the store with a crudely drawn map of how to get to Mike and Val's home supplied to me by three women customers competing with each other to help. Luckily, my hosts' home was not too far away—nor was it complicated to get there.

When I arrived Mike was nowhere to be seen nor had he phoned. Val and I chatted for a while then she showed me to my room. I was bringing my panniers in when Mike walked through the door. There was a slight bluster about him as we tried to figure out what had happened. Having pulled off the side of the road at the first intersection he admitted to being distracted by talking with a hitchhiker who'd asked for directions. He hadn't realized how speedy I must have been and how long he'd talked to the hitchhiker. Val nagged him about being more attentive. He insisted that I had arrived safely and that's all that mattered.

Over supper that evening I asked Mike if he knew of a good bike shop in town where I could get a tune-up. "David, my son, is a good bike mechanic. He'll probably do it for you. Let me phone him." Within half an hour my bike was on a stand outside David's garage. At 40 years of age David was still a keen mountain biker. He also worked part-time as a mechanic in a local bike shop. While he was swapping my tires around (the rear was showing some wear), checking and adjusting my gear cables and talking about our enjoyment of cycling, his wife Nicole and his three children arrived to say hello. Nicole, a nurse, was also an avid triathlete. We immediately swapped tales of our training schedules and compared our preferred equipment. Her bike—a Cervelo, was the same as mine. She wheeled the bike out, and, with an affection only other cyclists can appreciate, told how much pleasure she derived from riding it—even from just looking at it. David wouldn't take any payment for his thorough, hour-long tune-up. He said it would count as his contribution to the cause.

Day 17 Rest Day

This was not my first visit to Prince George. I emigrated from England in 1967 with my then wife Joyce and nine-month old Mia. Before I left England I'd been offered a teaching job in Prince George. So, from mid-August of 1967 to the end of June, 1969 I got to know BC's "Northern Capital" really well.

Mike and Val had suggested they give me a tour of the town. That would facilitate my visiting some places I wanted to see, doing a bit of supply shopping and land us at an afternoon potluck gathering being arranged by the local Parkinson's support group to acknowledge my fund-raising effort.

Most of the morning was taken up with a long interview with Mark Neilsen, a reporter for the Prince George Citizen, the major city newspaper and a television interview with CKPG, a local television station. Mark asked me what was my caloric output each day on the road. Although I hadn't thought about my calorie expenditure at all, I guessed between 4,000 and 5,000 a day based on what I knew of exercise and calorie burning. After the interviews I went into the house and weighed myself. I'd lost almost five pounds since leaving Whitehorse. To say I never felt hungry from time to time would not be true especially after many hours of riding each day. But, although I felt fit and had oodles of energy, I resolved to eat more.

When I left Prince George in 1969 it was a booming pulp mill town with a population of around 30,000. What I remember most was its sprawl, its pulp mill stacks belching sulphur-laden smoke (which, on a bad day smelt like rotten eggs) and the swirling waters of the Fraser and Nechako rivers as they met on the edge of town. It's still a sprawling community and the pulp mills and rivers still define the place. But its population has more than doubled over the past 43 years and the sprawl is much more extensive.

The first place I asked Mike to show me was the apartment building on Ingenika Street we lived in for a very short time when we arrived in the sweltering heat of late summer. It was a brand new building then and almost on the outskirts of town. My wife and I thought we were in the lap of luxury in that apartment. It had in-suite washer and dryer, a fridge and stove—appliances we thought would take years for us to afford. It even had central heating for God's sake! As we drove past the apartment (which was definitely not on the edge of town) I thought it had stood up well to the comings and goings of countless occupants and the harshness of Prince George's winter weather.

We drove past the school were I taught (it was no longer such but I remembered the building) and the hospital where my son, Daniel, was born. (We thought ourselves very avant-garde at the time with our MD allowing me to witness Daniel's birth.) I even recognized the hill were we'd go tobogganing on winter snow. The Inn of the North was the favourite watering hole for teachers on Fridays after school. It was then the only decent hotel in town but the beer parlour in its basement was a raunchy affair. Fistfights were common and you could buy beer from a server only while seated at your table. Bosomy women in fishnet stockings roamed the rowdy room selling cigarettes, chips and little packets of salted nuts. I'd gone a few times just for the spectacle but it wasn't a place I frequented often. The hotel was still a going concern but the beer parlour was long gone. Mike and Val, who had lived in Prince George since 1968, remembered the Inn's glory days and its reputation. We joked we could have been drinking next to each other on one of those Friday evenings 40-odd years ago.

I did my supply shopping on the way to a sightseeing tour of the impressive University of Northern British Columbia campus set on a hill northwest of town. The idea of a university in the town was just a twinkle in someone's eye when I lived there and now it's a world-class campus with over 4,000 students. It officially opened its doors in 1990 though much of its architecture looks a lot newer, with creative blends of wood, concrete and glass in both curvilinear and angular forms. Most of the campus buildings are clustered around the Agora (a Greek word meaning "gathering place")—a beautiful split-level courtyard.

By three in the afternoon Mike, Val and I were at the Parkinson's potluck gathering. A couple of dozen people were there, some of whom were sufferers while others were either spouses or family members. I managed to talk with everyone in the room and hear some of their stories of how the disease was affecting them. One woman, Carol, was determined to pursue as active a life as possible. She'd just returned from walking the Northumberland Coast Path on England's northeast coast. She looked fit and trim. I told her she was a great advert for staying vigorous at 66 whether or not with Parkinson's disease. We posed for photographs and before we all parted, the treasurer of the group presented me with a cheque for two hundred dollars as a donation to my fundraising ride. I was touched by the gift and thought how generous they were to contribute to a cause meant to help ameliorate the plight of all who suffer from the disease—including themselves.

That evening, over supper laced with wine, I got to know Mike and Val a little more. Val, a woman in her mid-seventies, had Parkinson's-like symptoms—hot flashes, diabetes and joint degeneration. Her knees bothered her and she, I could see, was not too nimble on her feet. She was waiting for both her knees to be replaced. As a young woman she'd spent two years working in Iran during the Shah's conflicted regime. Mike's taste for French berets and "Le Tour" was born when, one summer in his youth, he picked grapes in the Champagne region of France. "I've been wearing the berets and following the Tour ever since," he told me with a gentle pride in his voice. Seeing couples relating together is always an interesting experience and being with Mike and Val was no exception. Because of Val's relative immobility, Mike did most of the chores. He cooked the meals, did the shopping, cleaned house and generally saw to Val's needs. To say that he fussed around her would be too much but he certainly was attentive and there were numerous "terms of endearment" that passed between them. He seemed industrious by nature and had an abundance of energy that, for an eighty-one year-old, I thought rare.

Whether it was the wine or the mood was right, but Mike warmed to my question about religious beliefs. I can't remember what he'd said exactly that afternoon on our city tour, but it was about a church he used to attend. He told me he no longer had any affiliation with any church or faith for that matter. Over the past few years he'd become very disillusioned with organized religion and was slowly slipping from agnosticism to becoming a nonbeliever. I related a little of my journey, many years ago, from belief to atheism. I had studied theology as a young man, and it was that study, ironically, that had unmasked for me the hypocrisy between the declaration of belief and the acting of it in daily living. Growing older, the more I thought about belief structures of no matter what faith, it seemed that believing in them was the equivalent of admitting belief in ghosts and fairytales. Mike agreed when I concluded that the longer we live the more tenuous religious faith becomes.

Prince George to 70 Mile House (379 km)

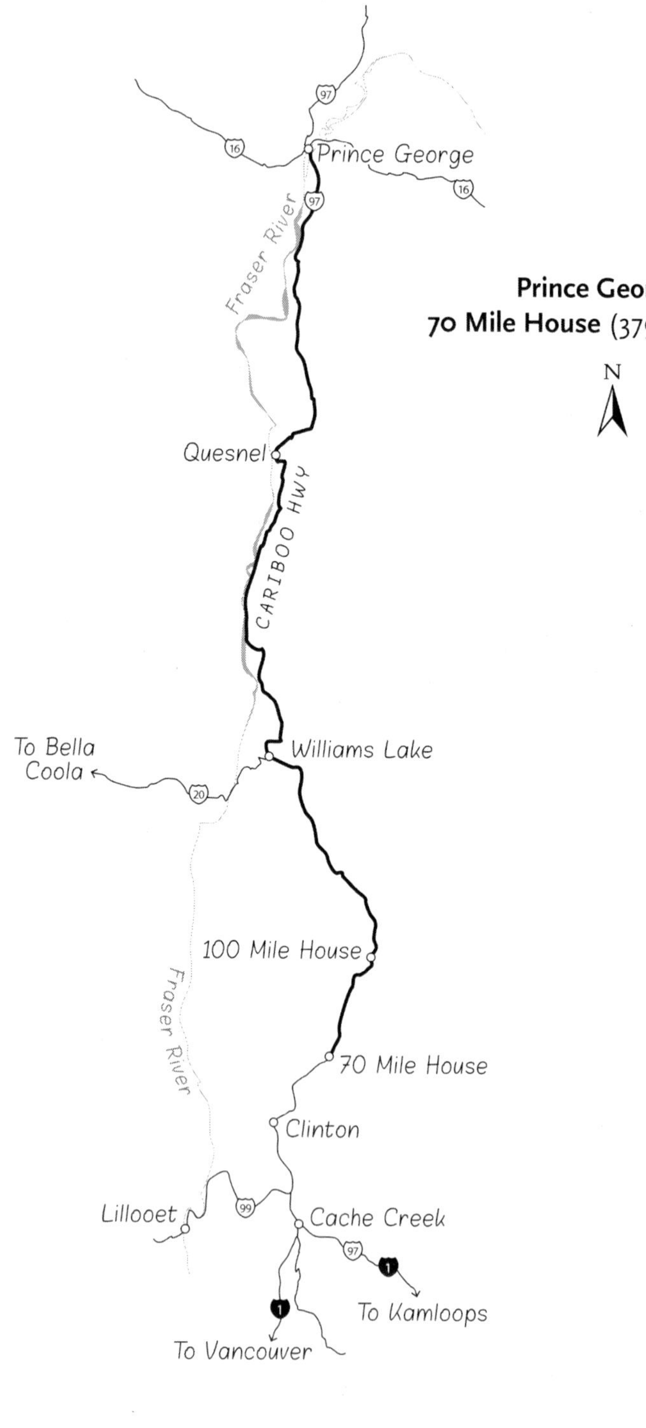

4 THE CARIBOO HIGHWAY (HIGHWAY 97)

Prince George to 70 Mile House

DAY 18 Prince George to Quesnel

By the time I was cycling over the Fraser River on the Simon Fraser Bridge leaving Prince George, I'd pedalled 1,636 kilometres in 14 days of riding. That's close to 117 kilometres a day. Not bad, I told myself as I began the long climb that confronted me once I'd crossed the bridge. Much better than my projected average of 100 a day. The morning's weather was perfect for riding—blue sky with patches of high cirrus, little wind and a temperature around 20 degrees. I was a happy cyclist that even hilly terrain couldn't disgruntle.

I stopped at a roadside store and café in the small village of Hixon and bought some orange juice and, after some hesitation, a packet of potato chips. I know that's a weird combination but I had suddenly decided to rehabilitate the lowly and maligned chip to a midday staple and I wasn't about to give up my preferred lunchtime beverage. The reason for this elevation of the chip (as you know, they're a post-ride favourite along with a cold beer) to become part of my lunch was my weight loss over the past two weeks. As I read the label on the chip package in the Hixon store I was impressed by the nutritional value of 75 grams of the thin, wavy, unevenly shaped shreds of potatoes the packet contained. There were all the ingredients I thought conducive to weight gain and my daily energy needs. Here's what the packet contained: 420 calories, 27 grams of fat, 500 milligrams of sodium, 39 grams of carbohydrate, 2 grams of fibre and 5 grams of protein. Not bad I thought for a bag of "Specially selected potatoes, vegetable oil, [and] salt." Admitted, the packet didn't carry the protein punch that a can of sardines does (18 grams) but it had five times more carbs than the sardines. It also had almost four times the total calories—420 versus 110. When I put the two together, I thought I'd have an all right lunch. (As the days progressed, I added a midday Coke to the mix. I thought my tummy would rebel but it didn't. And, in case you thought I wasn't including my daily fruit, I usually had a banana or apple in addition to my orange juice during the day.) Besides, averaging 117 kilometres of cycling a day carrying 55 to 60 pounds of "stuff" in my panniers, it was clear my body needed (I was going to say "deserved" but that might be going too far given my normal attitude to healthy eating) the extra calories no matter what their source.

There was a shady roadside park a few metres away from the store. I chose a bench among a clump of trees away from the traffic and munched on my newfangled lunch combo and listened to the rippling of a nearby creek. Whenever I had thought about my journey in the months before I started, I wondered whether I'd need a midday snooze. Over the last few years I've found it a refreshing thing to do especially after a hard morning ride. But no, so far I hadn't felt the need, which pleased me, and indicated my body was doing just fine. It wasn't long after leaving that secluded bench that I encountered a miserable hill that seemed to go on forever. It was one of those affairs that looked innocuous at first glance but its grade, though not steep, seemed to drag all the energy from my legs. I couldn't find my rhythm and it felt more like a fight against an intransigent foe than an upward slanting slab of asphalt.

Roadside signs told me I was in "Cariboo Country." What that meant exactly I didn't know. Highway 97 is also named the Cariboo Highway so I assumed all would be revealed as I pedalled south. One clue was another sign at the entrance to a long gravel road. It read, "Triple J Ranch, Trail rides, For That Real Cowboy Experience." I guessed one of its meanings was "Cowboy Country." I was certainly riding through lots of ranch-type countryside and by large dairy farms judging by the tall silos I saw in the distance. I imagined horses and riding were a big part of the culture in this part of the world. (Where I was heading the next day, Williams Lake, is famous for its summer rodeo or "stampede" as it's now called.) Evidence of logging was everywhere. Close to Quesnel I passed a sawmill, a pulp mill and several yards with logging trucks parked or being repaired. Logging was obviously part of "Cariboo Country."

The terrain was definitely "lumpy" for my whole day's ride and fortunately, as I neared Quesnel, the road dipped down toward the Fraser River giving me a long freewheel into town. On the long descent I noticed one of those large billboards on the roadside. Superimposed on a large Union Jack were the words "Wee Chippie. All you can eat for $12.95." There was no question about where I would be eating *this* evening. As soon as I saw the ad I could sense the hunger already building in my innards as I contemplated plate after plate of tasty, battery fish and not too crispy French fries swilled down with a couple of cold ones. "Wee Chippie," of course, is the Scottish rendition of "a small fish and chip shop," that renowned British institution some regard as the original fast food take-away. It didn't take me long to find the Fraser Bridge Inn and RV Park where I planned to spend the night. Luckily for me it was opposite the downtown area across the recently renovated Old Fraser River Bridge—a heritage pedestrian/bike thoroughfare. Unluckily for me though, its advertised campground was non-existent. The inn was surrounded by an asphalt parking lot. The next campground was 10 kilometres south of town and the lure of the Wee Chippie was too much for me to resist so I settled for a senior-discounted room at the inn.

Once I'd showered and changed I made my way back across the heritage bridge to the find the Wee Chippie. It was a couple of blocks away from the bridge's exit to downtown and I was there in no time. The cavernous restaurant was humming. As I arrived they decided to open up an extension to accommodate the suppertime crowd. The welcoming server showed me to an empty table by a window. Hum, I thought. Might take awhile before I get served. Not so. Within moments a young women came to take my order. She said I should help myself to the salad bar and that my order of two pieces of fish and plate of French fries would be served soon.

"And oh, can I get a pint of draught with that?" I said as she turned to leave.

"Sure. I'll be right back." I had just started my salad when my beer and fish and chips arrived. Trying to take my time over the first serving was impossible and I'd finished the plate in no time.

"Another for you sir?" The server knew my answer. I finished the second plate with the same gusto as the first. I caught the server's eye.

"Err. Do you think I could have another serving?"

"No problem sir. Can I get you another beer?" After five pieces of fish, three sides of French fries, all the salad I wanted, and two pints I left the place thoroughy satiated.

Outside, I found myself on the edge of Quesnel's downtown core. I had plenty of evening light left as I strolled the quiet streets of low-rise buildings back to my motel room. I looked for some reference to the Quesnellia Terrane I had read about when overlooking Simpson Peak near the Continental Divide two weeks ago but I found nothing. Perhaps it was too arcane or erudite to be written about or advertised on downtown Quesnel's information plaques. What I did discover was that Quesnel was an important part of the Cariboo Gold Rush of the 1860s. It was a terminus for paddle steamers (sternwheelers) bringing gold diggers and supplies heading east on the Cariboo Wagon Road to the epicentre of the "rush" in Barkerville some 80 kilometres from Quesnel. (Historically speaking, "Gold Rush" was another element of what is meant by "Cariboo Country.") The town developed into the commercial centre for the rush and, at the same time, established itself as a gateway to the north for river traffic. The town got its name from one of Simon Fraser's travelling companions, Jules Maurice Quesnel, a Montreal fur trader on Fraser's exploration of the Fraser River in 1808. (One of the original names for the river is Stó:lo—an name given it by the Stó:lo First Nation, the indigenous people of that area.)

Re-crossing the Fraser River heritage footbridge I stopped to admire its simple structure of wooden trusses and metal support beams. The bridge was originally opened in 1928 for pedestrians, horse-drawn vehicles and the occasional automobile. At 253 metres it was a longish span and needed constant upkeep. But by the early 1960s its increased use by heavy trucks made the bridge unsafe. The community petitioned the provincial government for a new bridge and in 1971 a new bridge crossing BC's longest river was opened. I could see from the recent renovations to the old bridge that most of the materials used were new but the concrete footings dated back to the 1920s. It's an impressive structure and I understand why the town now boasts that it's the "longest wood truss walking bridge in the world."

DAY 19 Quesnel to Williams Lake

Seeing the sign for Dragon Lake a few kilometres after I'd left Quesnel took me back to my first visit to the area forty-odd years ago. Friends in Prince George had invited my wife, Mia and me to their parents' cottage on the shores of that same lake for the weekend. It was to be our first taste of Canadian summer fun at the lake. We camped, we had wiener roasts by the campfire, we swam in the warm water of the small, shallow lake, we water-skied and ate coleslaw and potato salads on a picnic table in front of the cottage. I remember it as a happy time—a further initiation for us into Canadian family life. I also remember that as we were leaving in the early evening a huge bull moose crossed the road in front of us. It was our first large wildlife sighting since arriving in Canada the summer before. We couldn't have been more surprised or impressed by the stately animal with its enormous rack as it lumbered slowly into the roadside trees not even glancing our way. When we related the incident to our friends they told us tales of charging moose and of fatal accidents when cars ran into them on the highway. Yes, we were lucky to see the animal, they said, but they also told us we were just as lucky not to have run into the beast. The Dragon Lake of today, I saw, was much changed. Its neighbourhood is home, not to moose but to big-box stores and strip malls. Around the lake, instead of the odd lakeside cottage, there were large subdivisions cluttering the shore. As I rode by I mused that it was unlikely moose would come within a country mile of such suburban sprawl.

Riding south I became more and more aware of trains. Passing a cluster of buildings I caught up with a long CN freight train. The engineer was peering under the lead engine's front wheels as if inspecting for some defect. I called out hello to him. He turned and looked. "Anything wrong?" I shouted.

"No. Just checking. How far you come?" he questioned climbing back into his cab.

"Left Prince George this morning," I replied. Then. "Where you headed?"

"Be in Williams Lake tonight."

"See you there." I shouted. With that, he blew his whistle and trundled off giving me a friendly wave. I matched his speed for a while then he gained momentum and was gone. Around midday I saw the archetypical train scene. Off to my right a line of colourful freight cars pulled by three engines snaked and stretched their way along the reedy shoreline of a sizeable lake—water in the foreground, conifers as a backdrop. The train was so long I couldn't fit the engines and the last car in the same frame of my camera even at its widest of wide angles.

It was an unlikely place with an unlikely name where I stopped for lunch. It was the Fort Alexandria Café. Although there was a café, no fort was in sight. From the outside, the café looked decidedly run down with weathered cedar siding and fraying mosquito mesh at its windows and entrance door. Together with its hitching posts in front and a snake fence surrounding its yard it seemed a relic of yesteryear. Inside was a slightly different story. It was clean and spacious and had a large airtight stove at its centre. On one of the side walls was parked an ornate enamel and chrome wood-fired cooking stove covered with bric-a-brac and a collection of paperback local-history books. This was going to be my first prepared lunch on the road since I started my trip and although the menu was definitely not to my usual taste it assured large portions. Actually, I had no difficulty choosing something to eat. I ordered a toasted cheese sandwich and French fries.

I sat outside under a covered lean-to to eat. A tall, slim man came to sit at a nearby table. "Nice looking bike you got there. Where you heading for?" he asked.

"Williams Lake today. But I'm on my way home to Victoria."

"You'll know Salt Spring then?" He was a trucker who was born, raised and now lived on Salt Spring Island and knew Victoria well. I told him of my many trips to the island and my fondness for all the Gulf and San Juan islands. Driving his rig all day made him determined to stay in shape when not on the road. He loved to cycle, he said, and rode all the time when he was at home. "Definitely against stereotype," I joked. He smiled.

Before I left the café I browsed the books in the stove-top library. I learned that Fort Alexandria is a place not a building—in fact, it's a national historic site. There had been a fort established by the North West Company (which later became the Hudson's Bay Company) in 1821 and was named after the explorer Alexander MacKenzie. (Coincidentally, the word Alexandria, in its original Greek form, means "defender of men"—an appropriate name for a fort.) In 1793 he'd stopped there on his way south but was told by the First Nation villagers who lived there the river was too dangerous to proceed further. The fort thrived for a while as a wintering place for Hudson's Bay Company traders but it was the Cariboo Gold Rush that stimulated its rapid growth in the early 1860s. The fort became a large tent city of miners and a staging place for sternwheelers to travel up to Quesnel. The demise of the gold rush a few years later saw the end of the fort. Today, only this funky greasy spoon café with its fancy name remain.

Soon after leaving the café I heard a noise I was certain was a chain saw. There was no forest or woods close by, only a wooden workshop fifty metres ahead on my right. As I drew closer I saw a large wooden effigy of an erect grizzly bear in front of the workshop facing the road. The noise was of a chain saw all right, but it was not used to fell trees. Coming to a stop near the bear I saw, through an opening in the workshop, a man using the small saw fashioning what looked like another bear out of a cedar log. The man, realizing I was there, stopped sculpting, idled the saw and lifted his visor from his eyes and nodded hello. Realizing I didn't look like the buying kind, he put his head down and resumed working. As I was about to leave, a woman appeared from a side door and asked if she could help.

"Very lifelike," I said indicating the grizzly.

"Yes, he's very good." She nodded toward the sculptor.

Closer now to the beast I could see the detailed work the man had wrought. The shape of the arms and legs, the sharpness of the claws, the beadiness of the eyes and the position of the head in sniffing posture displayed the finesse of a skilled artisan.

"How's business?"

"Not bad. A bit quiet this summer for some reason."

"Perhaps the weather." I suggested, looking at the accumulating clouds.

"Could be. But you never know these days from one season to the next, especially since 2008."

Before I left, I asked if she'd take a photograph of me in front of the bear.

"This is the closest I'll ever get to a grizzly, I hope."

"They all say that."

Nearing the village of McLeese Lake, I realized I was travelling along what we'd now term "a communications corridor." On my right was the railway not more than 20 metres away. Another 20 or 30 metres from that was the river—the mighty Fraser. Within the space of 50 metres or so were road, rail and waterway. Not that the Fraser is used much these days—in the sense of a means of transportation, but its recent history tells of steamboat sternwheelers plying its waters from Soda Creek (a stone's throw from McLeese Lake) to Prince George and even to close to its source at Tête Jaune Cache. This all happened between 1863 and 1921—not too long ago. The Fraser at this point I was at is known as the upper Fraser. Below Soda Creek is the beginning of the treacherous waters of the Fraser Canyon—a stretch of river only used by adventurous river rafters and kayakers. The most famous part of the canyon is Hell's Gate, a narrow passage through which the already turbulent river squeezes. Simon Fraser famously described the spot as "a place where no human should venture for surely these are the gates of hell."

I was seeing signs for Williams Lake when the rain started—light at first then developed into a steady downpour. The long descent into Williams Lake was welcome as my speed approached 50 kilometres an hour. I'd be out of the rain soon, I told myself. The idea of setting up camp in the rain was definitely not appealing and the photographs I'd seen of the only campground I'd located in Williams Lake — the Stampede Campground, showed no trees or communal shelter. It was in fact on a large tract of land that adjoined the stampede arena itself and advertised itself more as a RV park than a place to pitch a tent. Definitely not to my liking.

I remembered staying at a small motel on the south end of town in the summer of 1998. I decided to give it a try—if it was still open. I recognized the tidy place right away. The Lakeview Motel. Set back from the road and surrounded by groomed bushes and flowerbeds, the place looked modest and comfortable in an old-fashioned way. I recognized the woman behind the desk (in what was more like a comfy living room than an office) as the one who had handed me my key thirteen years earlier. Mia and I had stayed there the night before I set off on a five-day, 500-kilometres bike journey through the Chilcotin country and Tweedsmuir Provincial Park to Bella Coola on the coast. (That's the trip that included my hair-raising ride down the Heckman Pass I recalled on leaving Burns Lake.) "Yes, I have a room available. I only have a double though," she replied when I asked for a room.

"Will that do?" I said I would take it. I told her about having stayed years ago and that I remembered her. I was hoping she'd say, "Oh, yes, you do look familiar." But no, she had no recollection of either Mia or me. The room was not large but its big window made it feel more spacious and, as one might expect from the motel's name, gave a view over Williams Lake itself. The room had a small kitchen so I was cooking my evening meal in no time. (Not before, I must say, walking a couple of hundred metres in the now light rain to a liquor outlet to buy my post-ride beer and chips.)

DAY 20 Williams Lake to 70 Mile House.

Looking out the motel window through the early morning drizzle to the lake below and the town spread out on its northwest end I found myself thinking what a bedraggled place the town looked. In sunshine, I'm sure it would appear better but it didn't seem to have much to work with. The town is built on a flat valley bottom and accommodates sawmills, railway yards, car lots, shopping malls, wide streets and highways all set side-by-side without much regard for aesthetics such as elegant buildings, quaint storefronts, trees, parks and other green spaces. As an acquaintance of mine said many years ago: "The trouble with North American cities and towns is they build the slums first and then think about the rest afterwards." What he was really alluding to was that many communities were built around industries (and often in BC, resource extraction) and that's what you see when you enter the place. So far, most of the towns on my trip fit that observation well.

The drizzle stopped as I was preparing to leave the motel.

So far, I'd kept to my riding schedule but now I realized I might have a problem sticking to it. Originally, my day's destination was to be 100 Mile House, a town 98 kilometres away. The following day I had planned to be in Lillooet—a 170 plus-kilometre jaunt. "I don't think so." I told myself. I knew I was feeling good, but not that good! Mulling the situation over, I decided I'd see how I felt at 100 Mile House and perhaps push on to 70 Mile House, 34 kilometres further on. That way I'd get a 130-kilometre day in and leave me 140 kilometres to ride from 70 Mile House to Lillooet the next day.

The morning's weather turned for the better and the drying landscape of rolling hills, small lakes and large groves of aspen looked lovely in the bright sunshine. By noon I was riding close to the shores of Lac la Hache, a longish lake lined with resorts and cottage homes. Soon after I saw the town of Lac la Hache's sign. I thought it would be a good place to stop, buy some fruit and find a nice spot to have lunch. After 10 kilometres of riding I still hadn't found a store or anything that looked like a town centre. Eventually, a couple of kilometres further, a gas station with a convenience store came into view. I stopped and asked where I'd find the town and a grocery store.

"This is it." The woman behind the counter said without a trace of irony.

"You mean there's no place to buy groceries?"

"Nope."

I couldn't believe it.

"Where do people do their shopping?" I asked.

"Williams Lake usually. Depends what they want. Some go to 100 Mile House."

There were a few staples in the store. I found some very ripe bananas and bought one. A little ways from the store I noticed a tidy stretch of grass with what looked like a well-preserved log cabin set back from the road. As I rode closer I read "Thrift Store" over the front lintel. A set of wooden steps led up to the door with the word "Closed" attached to it. I sat on the steps and ate lunch and then leaned back, eyes closed and enjoyed the warmth of the sun. Getting going again, it wasn't long before I came across a large and long roadside sign. It read: "Welcome to Lac la Hache—the longest town in the Cariboo." I estimated the township to be at least 15 kilometres long (the lake is 18 kilometres) and that's for a population of under 300 souls. No wonder there was no town centre or grocery store.

I arrived at the visitor centre of 100 Mile House as my watch showed three o'clock. I'd noticed the welcome sign as I'd coasted into town down the long approach road. "100 Mile House. Handcrafted Log Home Capital of North America" was artistically rendered on a huge laminated wood panel shaped, as you might imagine, like a log house. As I stepped into the beautifully constructed log building (of course) that was the visitor centre, a young guy asked if he could help.

"Do you know if there's a campground or motel in 70 Mile House?" I asked.

"Just a moment, let me ask." He turned and spoke to a woman sitting at a desk working at a computer. "This gentleman wants to know if there's accommodation at 70 Mile House—camping or a motel."

Speaking to me, she said, "There's no camping but there's the motel. Very basic though." After a few more questions from me about the place, I said that I'd probably stay there.

The guy looked at me and asked, "Would you like me to see if they've got a room? Could be busy at this time of year."

"Oh, that would be good." I returned.

He picked up the phone, found the number and dialed. After a sentence or two, he turned to me, "She's only one room left. If you'd like it, she suggests you book it now."

"How much?"

He repeated my question into the phone.

"Seventy dollars plus tax."

"Yes, I'll take it."

"She says she can only hold the room 'til six o'clock."

"I'll be there," I said knowing I could cover the 30-odd kilometres in far less than three hours. I thanked the guy for his help and went out to my parked bike.

The climb out of the town was steep and, although I wasn't in distress, I knew I was on a steady incline as I pedalled into the late afternoon. Actually, without knowing it, I'd been slowly climbing all day to the highest point on the Cariboo Highway—Begbie Summit, about an hour-and-a-half out of 100 Mile House. I came upon the sign at the brow of a long hill. It read: "Begbie Summit, Elevation 1232 m" (That's 4,042 feet in old money). That was why I seemed to be working hard all day.

I stopped to take a photograph of the sign. I looked at my computer and tripped it to total distance mode. I couldn't believe it. Showing was the number 2003. I knew I was getting close to 2,000 kilometres but not almost spot on. If my calculations were correct, I'd be home in only 500 kilometres. The summit was named after Matthew Begbie, BC's first Supreme Court judge. Before that he was an itinerant judge travelling throughout the province on foot and horseback. Unfairly to some, he was given the sobriquet, the "Hanging Judge" because he sent a number of men to the gallows. History, however, says he argued for (and won) clemency for many he thought wrongly convicted.

I didn't exactly "plunge" off the summit but I certainly made good time to 70 Mile House. The motel, simply named the 70 Mile Motel, was easy to spot and looked a little worse for wear. Apart from a gas station and convenience store directly opposite and three buildings less than 100 metres to the south, that's all I could see of 70 Mile House. The note on the motel office door directed would-be guests to the adjoining restaurant where the owner would be and where you could register. The Corral Restaurant was a simple affair—a long room with the kitchen in full view.

A large woman was cutting vegetable as I walked in. Smiling, she said, "You must be the one who phoned from 100 Mile House a couple of hours ago. I saw you ride in."

"Yes, I hope the room's still available."

"You're lucky. It's my last one. Been busy this weekend. Come on, I'll show where you're in." (It was a Sunday and the traffic had been fairly heavy.)

The room was small and simply furnished. The sink was in the room and the shower and toilet were crammed together in a small stall. At 70 dollars a night I thought it expensive but being the only show in town I assumed she could charge what she wanted. Before she left me in my room, she told me she was preparing a roast for the evening special (local beef she said) and I'd certainly like it. Thanking her, I said I'd probably pass.

DAY 21 70 Mile House to Lillooet

I woke early. Looking out the tiny window of the tiny bathroom of my room I could see dew heavy on the fields behind the motel. An ethereal mist hung low over all I could see. The morning sun shrouded the sky waiting, I was sure, to burn off the dampness and bring on a glorious day. I could make out the vague outline of a horse grazing in the field, swishing its tail against the first of the day's flies. By the time I was ready to leave at 7:30 the mist had lifted and the sun was as bright and as warm as I'd hoped.

My day's destination was Lillooet, a distance of 140 kilometres by my estimate. I was now heading into a different climatic zone—a semi-arid area that wouldn't change until I penetrated the Coast Mountains a couple of days away. If the normal pattern of weather held, I'd be saying goodbye to uncertain skies and rain and drizzle and be in hot temperatures with hardly a cloud in sight.

Presumably, I was 11 miles (17-plus kilometres) south of 70 Mile House when I came to the 59 Mile Roadhouse. As it was one of only two buildings for miles around I couldn't miss it. Initially, I thought it the original roadhouse built in the gold rush days of the early 1860s. But no, that building had burned down in 1948 and was, in fact, at a slightly different location. The current structure, while looking authentic, is a replica and was operated as a restaurant for many years before it closed its doors in 2009. Roadhouses were built as rest places for the hundreds of men (and some women) travelling north to the Cariboo gold mines. There were two routes to the mines: one starting in the Fraser Canyon at Yale; the other from Lillooet north of Yale. It was the route from Lillooet that was the mile zero for the mile markers that guided the men north. The roadhouses, constructed at about 12- to 14-mile intervals at a mile post, were essentially hotels and supply depots. Built where grass and water were plentiful and crops could be grown, they were indispensable rest areas for people and horses. A roadside plaque put this aspect of the gold rush succinctly:

To the Goldfields

In the 1860s the fabulous Cariboo goldfields were a lure for thousands. Miners, traders, and adventurers, many afoot, some with wheelbarrows, shared the pioneer route with mule train, plodding oxen, freight wagons and swaying stage-coaches.

Havens for man and beast were the roadhouses and stables every 12–14 miles along the way.

One of the delights of the last couple of days had been the intriguing and unusual place names. As a Brit, I'm used to weird place names. My favourite (though a tad gruesome) is Lower Slaughter in the English Cotswolds. (There is also an Upper Slaughter.) Stow-on-the-Wold is another in the same area. Now, riding south from Quesnel, I came across signs for Likely, Horsefly, Axe Lake (better known as Lac la Hache) and, just past the 59 Mile Roadhouse, Chasm. This latter place comprises only a few houses and is better known for the provincial park, Chasm Provincial Park, a few kilometres east of the highway.

I decided to phone Lorinda from the first settlement I came to with a payphone. I had called both Lorinda and Mia from Williams Lake but Lorinda was out. I wanted to tell her how much I missed her even though I was enjoying myself completely. It was in the Cariboo Lodge in Clinton, a small town on the southern edge of "Cariboo Country" where I found the phone. She was pleased to know I was still happily riding and no mishaps had befallen me. We talked about our rendezvous in Nanaimo in four days time. She, Mia and some of the Nanaimo Parkinson's support group were to greet me as I came off the ferry from Horseshoe Bay. We spoke of our excitement about seeing each other again and what a grand meal we'd have at our favourite restaurant in downtown Nanaimo.

An hour out of Clinton the topography and flora had definitely changed. The trees were predominantly pine—mostly Ponderosa, and the hills became spiky and strewn with rocks. Any flat ground was either pasture or under irrigation. And, with the change of scenery, my time on the Cariboo Highway (and Cariboo Country) was also about to end. Shortly before a road junction, a blue and white sign, too large to be ignored, told me I had a choice. "Your choice" it read. "Vancouver and Coast Cache Creek Hope Fraser Canyon via 1 Or Lillooet Whistler Scenic Route via 99." So, I was here. My mind and my route were already made up. Highway 99, the Sea-to-Sky Highway—the "Scenic Route"—was my path.

70 Mile House
to Nanaimo (410 km)
N
97
70 Mile House
Fraser River
Clinton
Hat Creek Ranch
99
97
Lillooet
To Vancouver
12
DUFFEY LAKE ROAD
To Lytton
Pemberton
Whistler
SEA-TO-SKY HWY
Squamish
Howe Sound
Horseshoe Bay
Ferry Route
99
1
Vancouver
Nanaimo
VANCOUVER
ISLAND
BRITISH COLUMBIA
WASHINGTON STATE, USA

5 The Sea-to-Sky Highway (Highway 99)

70 Mile House to Nanaimo

Swinging right at the junction of Highway 97 onto the 99 a slight quiver ran through me as I contemplated my next few days of riding. The sign I'd just passed didn't describe the route I was on as "scenic" for nothing. It is, as some might say, a "doozer" of a highway. (Meaning, of course, an extraordinary and difficult road—especially for a cyclist.) I've sometimes used the word "lumpy" to characterize my route south but what I was about to confront made the few 6, 7 and 8% grades I'd climbed over the past three weeks seem trifling. I knew what I was in for only because I'd driven the road a couple of times before and I was under no illusion about what lay ahead.

Two hundred metres after my turn was the famous Hat Creek Ranch, a large spread that goes back to the gold rush days. There were lots of cars and RVs in the parking lot so I assume it's still a going concern. I know that it's now a First Nation business and its attractions are a blend of First Nation and cowboy artifacts and activities. It looked rather picturesque, sitting as it does on a creek in the Bonaparte River valley, a few willows and cottonwoods shading some of the older buildings.

Although the air temperature was rising I felt comfortable. It was a pleasant change to be on my bike in just T-shirt and riding shorts after so many days of jacket and long sleeves. Riding through Marble Canyon Provincial Park, along the shores of Crown and Turquoise lakes, I saw many youngsters sunning themselves on floating air mattresses and others leisurely paddling canoes and kayaks. The steep walls of the limestone canyon, I imagined, would make the area oven-like by mid-afternoon when lake dipping would be the perfect antidote. I was enjoying the brightness and clarity of everything I saw as the road curved and weaved through the park, the light reflecting off the high, white limestone cliffs and the blue-green waters of the park's three lakes.

Exiting the park I began tracing the shore of Pavilion Lake, a much larger lake than either Crown or Turquoise. Nearing the entrance to a resort I noticed a man running by the roadside. One of his knees was bound by a substantial knee brace.

"You okay?" he shouted across the road.

"Yes. Why?" I shouted back.

He ran to my side of the road (in reality, it was more of a hobble than a run) and, nodding to my left knee, said, "What have you done to that knee? You come off?"

It was the first time on this trip anyone had made reference to my elastic knee support.

"No. It's just a compression sleeve. I've been wearing it for years."

I really didn't want to stop and chat so I kept pedalling albeit slowly. Undeterred, the guy ran/hobbled by my side all the while telling me how he'd not long ago had knee surgery but was determined to keep running and that (and this was the point of his tale) he'd cycled across the country a few years earlier. He slowed to a walk but continued shouting after me with his story. "The Fraser's just up the road. Good luck." were his final, shouted words as I pulled further away from him. I wondered what it was about him that made me not stop and talk. A little too manic, I thought. None-the-less, I still managed to feel guilty for being so unfriendly.

Not long after the "hobbling" man, I spotted something I've seen only rarely. Perched on top of a power pole was a hotchpotch of twigs and straw that is the signature of an osprey's nest. Getting closer, I could see the osprey. I stopped beneath the pole and took a photograph. The bird didn't budge. It looked imperiously down at me and then turned to survey the lake—a more fruitful direction from his point of view I imagined. I waited a moment hoping to see if it would spot something and take flight. Obviously, I thought, he was either satiated or being lazy. The idea that he might be just enjoying the scenery didn't occur to me until I rode off.

The early afternoon temperature was definitely rising. Limestone cliffs and pine forest gave way to scrubby range country with an abundance of sagebush and bunchgrass. There were few trees to offer shade along the rolling highway. Passing through the village of Pavilion I saw, in the distance, the land gently descending into what I hoped would be the drop-off of the eastern walls of the canyon of the Fraser River. I rode on; my eyes glued to the mountains ahead, mountains

I knew formed the far side of the canyon. Yet the river itself remained elusive. What I thought was just around every bend seemed forever in the distance and out of sight. Finally, the scrubby terrain began to look tamed and cultivated. Large fields of lush, green alfalfa stretched out to the edge of what I envisioned to be the cliffs that plunged to the river's swift waters. I was right. Suddenly, it came into view. Rounding a descending bend I could see, less than a kilometre away, the angrily swirling and muddy waters of a river you instinctively knew was mindlessly and utterly malevolent. The precipitous canyon walls hung like giant claws pawing at the seething torrent. It was a spectacular and stunning sight—frightening in its power. I could feel the muscles of my face form a wide smile. "Glorious," I said out loud. "How majestic." I was looking at one of the world's great rivers. And I was seeing it doing what it has been working at for millennia: chiselling a deep and wide channel through the surrounding mountains, mountains that are the foothills of the Cascade and Coast ranges.

The fertile cutbanks I was now riding along I could see disappearing into a narrowing gap of the river's gorge. Descending another steep hill I came across two cyclists stopped on the other side of the road. They were collecting and purifying water from a trickle seeping from the roadside bank. I rode over and we began talking. They were young Belgians—one from Ghent, the other from Liège, on a three-week bike tour of southern BC and the Rockies. They had left that morning without adequate water. Because of the heat of the day, they'd almost run out. Using their water-filtering gadget, they were making hard work out of collecting and then filtering the meager amounts slowly filling their water bottles. They had sweated hard coming out of Lillooet so I knew I'd have some good down hills ahead although, they assured me, there were some really steep up hills.

The river and its canyon were mesmerizing. I couldn't keep my eyes off them, so entranced I almost missed a grazing mountain sheep off to my right. I braked hard and stopped in time to photograph the graceful animal before it bounded across the road and disappeared into the rock-strewn hillside.

After sweating up a particularly long and steep hill (my second 10%er) the road levelled out to offer the welcome site of the Fountain Flat Trading Post & Gas Bar. I'm sure the place had been here for years but the present structure was a brand new, "fully air conditioned," log building. It sat under the pinnacles of craggy mountains on a high bench with the river not too far away. The store's sign displayed, in red neon, "35.0°C." Too hot for comfort for me. Inside I bought and guzzled down two bottles of orange juice before stepping out of its cold cocoon into the hot sun. I was glad to be on the bike—a least the wind kept me a little cooler.

The river played peek-a-boo for a few kilometres until I began a long descent onto a wide, flat bench-like plain where I saw it, once again, slicing through the surrounding land. I stopped at a viewpoint overlooking the scene. A large sign read, "Lillooet Guaranteed Rugged." What that was supposed to mean I had no idea. But what I now knew was the settlement in the distance was Lillooet and I'd be there within the half-hour.

Nearing the town the road flattened and, for the first time since passing through McLeese Lake two days earlier, I was riding alongside the Fraser—now wider and calmer than a few kilometres back. I came to an intersection. To turn left was to head to Lytton. To turn right led to the bridge into Lillooet—my direction. (In the meteorological world of Canada, Lytton and Lillooet are the nation's hottest communities. Mere fractions of a degree separate them on the hottest days of the year. In 1941, they both recorded 44.4°C, a Canadian record.) After crossing the bridge over the river I turned right into the town's only campground—the Cayoosh Creek Campground. It was a nice enough place—grass campsites, large, clean washrooms and showers. But as I looked toward the town I could see a steep and uninviting hill that lead to the town centre. That was where the stores, restaurants and motels were. I was tired, hot and sweaty. After 140 kilometres of riding did I really want to set up camp, cook a meal, take a shower and then ride or walk into town up that mountain of a hill to shop for groceries and make my phone calls? No. I didn't. Let's get the hill out of the way first, get into town, find a cheap motel, cook a meal there and settle down to an early night and rest my tired body. That's what I told myself—and that's precisely what I did.

Luckily, the 4 Pines Motel was no more than half-a-kilometre from the top of the short but steep hill into town. It was a modern looking motel with white siding and green trim—a two story L-shaped building. They had a large room on the ground floor for 59 dollars a night. I thought it a steal. Before I settled in I walked the few blocks to a grocery store in search of beer and chips. Not since Jake's Corner had I wanted a cold one with such relish. After my supper I phoned Lorinda and Mia and then Marcia, Mia's oldest friend, who lives in Pemberton and on whose lawn I would pitch my tent tomorrow evening. I told Lorinda how I was looking forward to seeing her in Nanaimo and to riding back to Victoria together. She's a strong rider and I joked that I would be hanging off her wheel all the way home. "I doubt it," she scoffed. But I knew that would be the reality.

Lying on the motel bed staring at the wiggly line of a road on my map I began to conjure up my next day's hard ride. I was thinking of how I used to feel the night before a marathon. I would go through every aspect of the course in my mind, visualizing how I would handle the discomfort and then the pain that would be my constant companions from the halfway point until the finishing line. The final 10 kilometres would be the worst—my mind's mind and my body's mind battling each other for dominance. Although both were highly trained, it would be the mind's job to push the body to its limits no matter how painful and how strident were the signals for it to quit. Toward the end, the dichotomy of my two minds would reach a kind of desperation. My disciplined mind would cajole, even bully, my body's seductive, almost pleading voice—"All you need to do is stop and this pain and horrible effort will go away." "No way." My mind would counter. "The finish line is just up the road. Come on." Then, "You can't let all your hard work over months of training go for naught now. You're almost there for Pete's sake!" This internal conflict would go on until the race's end when I'd walk in a daze revelling in the feeling of not hurting any more.

Tomorrow's ride, I knew, would be my journey's marathon. I was going to hurt my body in a way reminiscent of my racing days. And like those days, I was looking forward to the challenge, not of the distance so much, but of the terrain—the steep grades that epitomize the Duffey Lake Road, the most difficult part of my present highway and, without doubt, my whole journey. It would be the crux of my three-and-a-half-week ride—a kind of climax, in literary terms, from which the dénouement would quickly unfold. This all sounds masochistic I know, but it was my natural way of anticipating something I knew would be both difficult and gratifying. I would feel dread and excitement almost simultaneously. My two minds would, once again, be fully engaged.

DAY 22 Lillooet to Pemberton

I left the motel early. I wanted to avoid as much of the day's heat as possible. Sailing down the town's hill I turned sharply right to follow the narrow, rolling Highway 99 toward the walls of rock the road was about to penetrate. Not too far on, in front of a small gas station, was a sandwich board. It read. "Last Service for 100 km." I looked down at my water bottles. Full. Although the sign was ominous, I'd be fine I told myself. The morning sun was still hidden by the eastern hills and my plan of starting my ride west through the mountains before its rays rose over their tops was working.

The grand Seton Lake came into view at about five kilometres. It stretched blue and clear into the distance. I stopped to take a photograph and to peer at the road curving up on its left shore. I could see a camper van slowly descending the long and very steep incline. The driver pulled into the small parking area of the lake's viewpoint where I was standing. He got out with an anxious look on his face and touched his front tire. I could smell the smell of burning brake drums. So could he.

Moving toward the rear tires he turning to me and said, "Going up there?"

I nodded, "Yes."

" Good luck."

He muttered something else as he continued his inspection but I missed it. (Probably, "You must be crazy!") I was back on my bike and pedalling off. "Better get on with it." I thought.

Within 50 metres of leaving the parking area I was out of the saddle and within moments of doing that I was gasping for air. Since I first thought about my journey down the length of the province I'd had this section of road in my mind. And the word I feared most, the one that became, in my mind, synonymous with the road, and the one I never wanted to utter was "walk." To walk would mean I had surrendered. It would mean I had gotten off my bike and walked because the climb had become too difficult. It would mean my mind had succumbed to my body. In fact, I would only refer to it as the W-word as if to deny it credence.

Starting the climb the W-word had already entered my mind.

My strategy, always, when on a steep uphill grade, is to gear down gradually as the slope gets more acute, trying to save my easiest gear until the very top. What I want to avoid is spinning my pedals too quickly too soon so wasting energy. (To spin too early is akin to treading water in a pool—staying afloat but not moving too far. Or, in the vernacular, "Going nowhere fast.") With this first climb, I was into my easiest gear almost immediately and I was nowhere near spinning—the grade being so severe. Over years of touring with panniers on my bike I've become adept at pedalling while standing. Now, I was out of the saddle as an instinctive response to the steepness. My heart sank as I thought of the six kilometres that lay ahead and I had only just started with no easier gear left. Not only that, the steepest pitch—a 13% gradient, was at the very end.

My notion of letting the slope dictate the progression down through my gears was almost pathetic. It assumed I had some control over the process. In reality I was at the mercy of the hill. I struggled up the first ramp, fighting for breath. "Keep calm." I began my self-talk. "Let the breathing smooth out." I knew as I settled into a rhythm my breathing would become manageable and standing as I pedalled would open up my chest allowing my lungs to get more oxygen. But I could only stand for so long before my quads began to burn. I was still in shade but I was sweating profusely. An older model truck chugged slowly past me. Its smelly, oily exhaust distracted me for a moment until it disappeared up the road. I pushed on, in and out of the saddle. Cresting the first grade the road gave a little dip before resuming its inexorable climb. I still hadn't stopped. I still wasn't walking.

The next ramp began after a tight switchback and seemed to disappear around another. Although this second long ramp was at 11% I was determined to best it. And I did. Sweating hard and breathing even harder, I pedalled my way higher. The W-word was my constant companion now but I wouldn't give in. "Any moment now. Any moment." I thought. But I ignored the temptation. My other mind telling me, "Keep going, keep going. Don't give up. You can do it, you can do it." My stubborn self was prevailing...so far.

Still on my bike, I pressed on. I was uncertain when the final 13% grade would present itself. The W-word ran interminably through my mind. It would not go away. Another sharp hairpin bend and I knew I was on it. The grade was nothing like anything I'd experienced on this trip before. It seemed perpendicular compared to what I'd just ridden. Once I stood up I knew I wouldn't sit again no matter how my quads howled. Rocking my bike from side to side I trod on my pedals like treading through mud. Despite the weight of my body over the front of my bike I could feel the front wheel becoming lighter and lighter as if wanting to become airborne as the pitch steepened. I was breathing and working harder than ever. I dared not look up. I didn't want to know how much further I had to go. Pain and fatigue were accumulating fast. "How long can I stand this? How long can I go on?" I began to doubt myself. Then it happened. The road didn't go up anymore. It was over. I'd crested the hill still on my bike. The dreaded W-word had been vanquished. "Well done Crouch. You did it." I congratulated myself out loud. If anyone had seen and heard me at that moment would they have thought me crazy? I don't know. I felt like a king.

No, I didn't fall off my bike and collapse in a heap on the side of the road. I didn't even stop to rest. I was so elated I just kept pedalling. But not for long. In less than 10 metres I was freewheeling down a long, winding slope with a big, wide grin on my face.

Soon after my descent off the "The Hill" I stopped at the BC Forest Service recreation site delightfully named Cinnamon to eat an energy bar and re-hydrate. It was a lovely spot on the banks of Cayoosh Creek—a body of fast-flowing water looking more like a river than a creek. This was the same creek running through the campground I almost stayed at in Lillooet. It drains out of the high Cayoosh Range, through Duffey Lake and into the Fraser at Lillooet. Sitting on its banks thinking about what I'd just done made me think of Ken Chlouber's pithy two liner: "You are better than you think you are. You can do more than you think you can." Ken is a founder of the Leadville 100 Trail Run—a brutal 100-mile mountain race in Colorado. He thinks the answer to pain and fatigue toward the end of a race can be summed up in one word, "digdeep." When it was pointed out to him "dig deep" were two words, he replied, "No it's not. It's one word, "digdeep." I had certainly "dugdeep!"

The Duffey Lake Road is not one that flattens out or travels in a straight line so most of my morning was a series of hills and curves. I pedalled on passing through magnificent scenery—the road following the narrow Cayoosh Valley. I was surrounded by snow-capped peaks in every direction and, never more than a few metres away, the turbulent waters of the creek kept me company. I lost that company when the valley broadened and the shores of Duffey Lake came into view and the creek disappeared into its deep waters. Towering mountains, some over 2,500 metres (8,000 ft), flanked the long and graceful lake. Toward the west the glaciated and icefield heights of the Cayoosh Range rose skyward, mottled with rock and ice.

I didn't realize as I rode on I was gaining elevation with every passing kilometre and by the afternoon I was riding through sub-alpine terrain. Gone was the semi-arid flora. I saw lupin, fireweed, tansy and Indian paintbrush again, even daisy and dandelion. The roadside was lush with the greens of grasses and shrubs. Hemlock, spruce, fir and spindly pine replaced the aromatic Ponderosa.

Up ahead a truck had stopped. Laying a few metres in front of it I saw something black. I knew immediately it was an animal but I didn't know what. Getting closer I thought it might be a wolverine—it was about the right size. But no. As I drew nearer I recognized it as a bear cub. A passing vehicle must have hit it. Blood was seeping from its mouth onto the road as its life ebbed away. It looked strangely comfortable lying on the warm pavement. One of the two men in the truck told me it had just happened. The truck that hit it hadn't stopped. He'd called the conservation officer in Pemberton and she was on her way. I felt ill at ease getting my camera out and photographing the dying animal. I rationalized my act with a "That's life." Tennyson's "Nature, red in tooth and claw" flashed through my mind but that was not apropos of this scene. Animals are often no match for speeding vehicles.

Passing the entrance to the Joffre Lakes Provincial Park I knew I'd soon be flying down the Cayoosh Pass to the level road paralleling Lillooet Lake. The not-so-subtle road sign warned of what I was about to negotiate. "Caution Extreme Grades Next 13 km" it read. On my road bike, downhill are my delight. I regularly touch speeds of 60–65 kph. Once I topped out at 81 kph coming down the Strathcona Parkway, the approach road to the Mt. Washington ski hill three hours north of my home in Victoria. It was the fasted I've ever been on a bike. On my touring bike I'd be far more circumspect.

Plunging down the winding pass was a pure rush. The tight hairpins precluded speeding and I was careful not to brake too hard or too often. A couple of motorbikes roared past me on their way up. Nothing passed me on the way down—probably because I was going faster than any vehicle. The grades were just as steep as my morning's tussle out of Seton Lake. Then I saw the yellow and black sign. "15%" it read. (BC's Ministry of Transportation only indicates grade percentages on the downhill slopes.) Years ago, when I first encountered this hill in my car, I passed a young couple pushing their loaded bikes up this incredibly steep pitch. The road had just been paved and no signs were up. Now I knew why they were walking. Although I met no traffic going my way, the acrid smell of burning brake linings hung in the air. A semi-permanent aroma on the hill, I imagined. At the bottom I checked my computer. I'd maxed out at 63 kph.

It was a 10-kilometre ride along the perfectly flat road to my day's end in Pemberton. I passed by the First Nation village of Mount Currie. I gave a friendly wave to teenagers swimming and floating in large inner tubes on the Lillooet River. They waved back their hello.

While in Lillooet, I'd arranged with Marcia (Mia's friend) to meet at the junction of Pemberton's main street and the highway. I said I'd be there at 4 p.m. I was bang on time. Five minutes later Marcia and her young daughter, Abby walked across the road to greet me. I hadn't seen Marcia for perhaps twenty years or more, but I recognized her immediately. She lived, with her husband Bob, Abby and their little mutt, Charlie, 7 kilometres north of town. I loaded my panniers into her SUV, she took off home and I followed on my (light-weight!) bike, trying to remember her directions.

Before I showered and changed, Marcia presented me with a bowl of tortilla chips and a beer.

"Mia said you'd like these." Marcia said as she drew up a chair at the kitchen table.

"Glad she told you that. These have been my treat of choice over the past three weeks, that's for sure."

We chatted for a while. She and Mia hadn't seen each other for years she told me, but was thrilled to hear from her and catch up on old friends. She was happy to help in my fund-raising ride.

We'd arranged I'd pitch my tent on their lawn. It's an easy tent to erect and I was finished in no time. Abby was practising tightrope walking on a rope tied around two stout maples opposite the tool shed and suspended about half-a-metre off the ground. She was a tall, spare youngster and any physical awkwardness she was feeling in her puberty years was being countered by her balancing act. She was enjoying school holidays, she told me, but was missing her friends. Ah, the joys of rural living.

Before I said good night, I made two phone calls: one to my son Daniel; the other to Leslie—a woman I'd never met who was the executive director of the Squamish Renaissance Retirement Settlement. Daniel was coming from Vancouver to meet me in Squamish. We'd been planning for him to ride with me to the ferry terminal in Horseshoe Bay—a 45-kilometre ride away. He, Becca, my daughter-in-law and my two grandchildren, Hailey and Emmett would be there in two days time. Mia and Betty Hum had somehow arranged with Leslie for me to stay at her retirement residence the night I was in Squamish. Leslie, and a guy named Brian, would be waiting for me in front of MacDonald's in downtown Squamish at 5 p.m. I wouldn't miss them, she assured me.

Crawling into my sleeping bag I couldn't have been more content. I'd had an exhausting but exhilarating day's ride through scenery that was both beautiful and grand. I hadn't walked. I'd arrived at Marcia and Bob's on time. I'd had my beer and chips. I was clean. I'd had a tasty meal with generous people and now I was sleeping in my tent again.

Day 23 Pemberton to Squamish

Bob, Marcia's husband, had succinctly described the highway between Pemberton and Squamish as, "Uphill from here to Whistler; downhill from Whistler to Squamish." I was about to find out how accurate that was. I had no reason to doubt his word—it was mountain country after all and officially called "The Sea-to-Sky Highway." But my caveat is: Never trust a non-cyclist to be realistic about how hilly or flat a road might be. Nor how far the next town is.

As usual, I was on the road fairly early. I'd had a fine breakfast with Marcia, Bob and Abby before we all said our goodbyes and I left their cozy and trim little house in the country. The flat Pemberton Valley soon began to buckle as I turned onto the highway and headed to my lunch date with myself in the fancy ski- resort town of Whistler. I hadn't been to Whistler for many years and I was curious to see how it had changed. It's about 35 kilometres from Pemberton to Whistler and most of the road was lumpy and, as Bob had predicted, a goodly portion was uphill. The sun and blue sky made the morning very agreeable although a fairly strong head wind made my work on the uphills that much harder.

Despite my arduous Duffey Lake Road ride of yesterday, I felt little ill effect. Okay, my quads were a bit tight and they told me so on some of the steeper grades. But apart from that, I felt my usual self. It's as if my mind keeps saying to my body, "Let's go." And my body responds with, "Okay, I'm up for it. Which way?" All my adult life, particularly as a competitive athlete, I've been amazed at the recuperative abilities of the body. On this trip, each riding day, my mind and body have revelled in being on the bike and pedalling home pain free (notwithstanding the Duffey Lake Road!).

Entering Whistler I rode past one of those welcome signs that has a sniff of pretension. "Whistler" it proclaimed, was the "Host Mountain Resort" of the "2010 Olympic & Paralympics Winter Games" Underneath those words was "Bienvenue." Apparently, understanding French was a condition of being welcomed. Fifteen minutes later, I was sitting under the umbrella of an outdoor café ordering a tuna sandwich and juice. At the next table a family of three were trying to make an order in their faltering English. Judging by the conversation between them they were French. The server had difficulty understanding them even when they asked for *les pommes frites*. So much for "Bienvenue."

Whistler was a much bigger community than I'd recalled. Spreading out into the surrounding forest, hills and lakes it looked very prosperous. But the core of what is referred to as "the Village" hasn't changed that much. Although it has a faux-Swiss alpine resort feeling, I enjoyed looking at the tourists poking about the streets and the young locals pedalling their beat-up bikes and leaving them willy-nilly to go chat with friends. The atmosphere was relaxed and time unimportant: a bit of a contrast to my long solo journey.

Bob was also right about it being mostly downhill to Squamish from Whistler although there were some significant ascents. Lorinda and our friend Patti were training to do the GranFondo Whistler, a long distance bike ride from Vancouver to Whistler in early September, and had asked me to take note of the terrain between Horseshoe Bay and Whistler. They already knew there was a net elevation gain of 700 metres (2,296 ft) from Vancouver to Whistler but they were curious to know what that looked like on the road. I was going to have to tell them it looked pretty ugly.

They could be distracted from the grueling grind, however, by the splendour of the mountains either side of the road. Leaving Whistler the dark obelisk of Black Tusk jutted into the sky. Further west was the 2,678-metre (8,786-ft) Mt. Garibaldi and the glorious panorama of the Tantalus Range stretching northward. No, there wouldn't be a dearth of spectacular scenery if, and that's a big "if," they had the spare energy to sightsee.

My occasional companions on my ride south were the

Cheakamus River and the CN Rail line. I was pleased to see both. I was hoping to snag a photograph of a kayaker or two on the river (that's what it's known for—kayaking) but I saw none. As for the railway, I did see a work crew repairing the line (complete with a diesel rail car)—and I did get a photograph of it.

The road flattened out completely about 10 kilometres from the town of Squamish itself. Either side of the highway were the large suburban settlements of Brackendale and Garibaldi Heights. I knew I was nearing the town when I could see the cliff face of The Chief—a world-famous climbing wall that looks down on the town from the south. It's a 700-metre (2,296-ft) high piece of granite, reputedly the second largest in the world. I immediately thought of my friends Jeffrey and Zachariah. They're climbers and often come from Victoria to scale The Chief's numerous routes. I looked at the rock with new eyes. Now I know what they're up against.

I met Leslie and Brian as planned at 5 p.m. They were waiting, with their bikes, to escort me to the retirement home. Leslie zoomed off ahead of me with Brian on my wheel. Suddenly she stopped and waited for us to catch up.

"We have to stay here for three minutes. We can't be too early."

I hadn't a clue what she was referring to. She looked at her watch and then reached into her only pannier and pulled out what I thought was a bullhorn. Looking at her watch again, she thrust the thing in the air and, after a pause, pulled the trigger. It let out a screeching blast into the late-afternoon air.

"Now we can go. Follow me." And off she scooted toward a large building halfway down the block.

We pulled into a parking lot in front of a high portico to a new four-story building. Brian and Leslie let me go ahead.

Before I knew it, a small crowd emerged from the portico and began clapping and cheering. They were welcoming me.

Someone took my bike as people I'd never met before gathered around me. A young woman and a slightly older guy, both holding notepads, introduced themselves as reporters. They asked questions, interview-style, about my trip, how I was feeling and about why I was riding for Parkinson's. After the questions, the woman said, "I'm Rebecca. We spoke together when you were in Vanderhoof. It's so good to see you in person." We chatted some more and then Leslie interrupted to put a glass of beer in my hand. "Mia said it's one of your favourites. And there's more upstairs." It was a beer brewed in Squamish by Howe Sound Brewing. Its Devil's Elbow pale ale is really good. I took a long sip.

"Close your eyes and listen to my voice. Who do you think this is?" said a woman behind me.

"Don't ask me that. I haven't a clue. There're so many people here I've never met before." I felt awkward. This person obviously thought I'd recognize her by her voice. I had closed my eyes but opened them again when she said,

"It's Betty, Betty Hum from Vancouver. You know, from Parkinson Society BC."

I'd never met Betty but over the months before my trip we'd spoken often on the phone about the logistics of my fundraising effort—how to instigate it; what it would entail; where I might stay. What I appreciated most about Betty was her reassurance that, no matter how much money I'd raise, in her eyes I'd be successful. When I spoke of my fear that I wouldn't raise a cent, she calmed me with, "John, don't worry about the money. You'll be raising awareness of the disease and that's a lot." We gave each other a big hug as if we were old friends. She looked lovely in a black summer dress that matched her long black hair and contrasted with her clear, pale skin.

Betty turned and introduced a tall, elegantly dressed woman. "This is Ursula, she's from the Squamish Parkinson's support group, and in fact she started it." When Ursula spoke I instantly recognized her as English. She and her husband Neil had arrived in Squamish a couple of years earlier straight from England. They were disappointed no Parkinson's support group existed in the town. Ursula's mother had died from the disease and she was determined to raise awareness of its deadly effects. The support group she started a year earlier held its monthly meetings at the retirement settlement. When Betty had told her I was passing though Squamish she had asked Leslie if I could stay in the facility's guest suite. Ursula told me that my effort was just the thing the society needed to get the press's attention. She was thrilled, she said, that the local newspapers were picking up my story.

After being introduced to several other people, Leslie, an exuberant woman, led me into the building's foyer.

"Leave your bike and stuff here. I want to introduce you to the residents. They're having supper in the dining room." Leading me down the hall she continued, "They've heard all about you and are really looking forward to meeting you." There were about 40 or 50 eating in what could have been a fancy restaurant. Leslie announced to the room that I was the guy whom she had told them about. The one who'd cycled all the way from the Yukon to raise money for Parkinson's disease. There was some applause and someone shouted, "Aren't you tired?"

"A little," I replied. I thanked them and Leslie for their welcome and added, "I need to get a shower soon else no one will come near me." Leslie took my cue and led me back to the foyer.

Before Leslie showed me to my room, Ursula invited me for supper at the local favourite eating and drinking hole—the Howe Sound Brewery Inn, with Neil, Brian and his wife, Leslie and Lisa, the residence's manager. We'd meet at 6:30 in the foyer.

My room, by my standards, was luxurious. I could have been staying at the Vancouver Fairmont. It had two bedrooms each with its own en suite, a full kitchen, a dining area, a balcony and a large living room. On the dining table was a basket full of chocolates, potato chips and fruit. In the fridge were bottled water and two quart-size bottles of Howe Sound Brewery's Devil's Elbow. I couldn't believe the generosity and such hospitality that Leslie had showered on me. As she left she said, "If you need anything else, just call reception, they'll help you. And, oh, if you want to phone Mia or anyone, just help yourself." I was at a loss to express my gratitude. This was completely beyond anything I might have expected.

With my bike parked on the balcony, my panniers partially unpacked and my body feeling refreshed after a long shower, I sprawled on the ample chesterfield and phoned my son Daniel. We arranged we'd meet in the foyer at 10 the next morning. Becca and the kids would be there to accompany us as we rode together to Horseshoe Bay. On the phone with Mia, she needed to know what ferry I proposed to take. She and Lorinda, along with the Nanaimo Parkinson's support group, would be meeting me at the Departure Bay terminal. I said I'd be on the three o'clock sailing.

The meal with my hosts was thoroughly enjoyable. Even though we'd just met, the conversation was easy and interesting. I managed to eat a whole large pizza with no problem.

"Edgie Veggie" it was called. Of course, it went down very well with a pint of the house's special brew. It was about 8:30 when we said our farewells. I would see Leslie in the morning. She'd invited me for breakfast with the residents.

DAY 24 Squamish to Horseshoe Bay

Daniel, Becca and my grandchildren were talking with Leslie when I walked down the stairs into the foyer. There were lots of hugs and kisses. I was so pleased to see them all. We went up to my room—I wanted to show them how well I'd been looked after. Hailey and Emmett romped into every room until their eyes settled on the chocolates and chips still sitting on the table. Yes, of course they could have some, I told them indulgently. As long as their Mummy approved, I cautioned. Poor Becca. What was she going to say? With a packet of chips and a few chocolates in their hands we returned downstairs, Daniel carrying my panniers while I handled my bike.

The sun was out as I said goodbye to Leslie, Lisa, Ursula and Neil (to my surprise they had come to wave me off) and some of the staff. Because Daniel was on his much lighter and therefore faster road bike, I decided to put my panniers in Becca's car for her to take to the ferry terminal at Horseshoe Bay. That way it wouldn't be such a chore for Daniel and me to ride together at the same speed.

Riding beside my son always gives me that feeling of contentment and connectedness a father can feel with his adult children. Today was no exception. Daniel's bike is the one I'd given him a few years ago. He'd expressed interest in using cycling as part of his fitness regime. I was happy to give him my good "second" bike both as encouragement and as another way of being together—just him and me. For a number of years now, when we have family gatherings on Pender Island, we'll often go riding together, touring the island and challenging each other on the stiff and punchy hills the island is noted for. So, once or twice a year we ride together and it's always part camaraderie, part familial intimacy and part competition. This day's ride would definitely not include the latter.

Through all the imperfections of my fatherhood, with my son the one constant has been introducing him into my world of physical and athletic endeavour. Even before Daniel's birth I came to understand that part of being a father is to present his offspring to the wonders (and vagaries) of the physical world. As only a parent can do, when Daniel was barely four, I inducted him into the perils of traversing a swollen stream on a fallen tree in a wooded park (much to his mother's consternation). That was a good start. Years later, we uncovered the vastness and mysteries of the southern California deserts together. We still recall with a chuckle the afternoon, while climbing a steep and boulder-strewn gully in Joshua Tree National Park, we were startled when Daniel almost trod on a curled-up rosy boa, a beautiful desert snake, semi-concealed between the rocks. When he took up distance running in his late twenties I was delighted and proud. He and Mia had supported me at countless races over the years. Now it became my turn to cheer him on and offer encouragement.

We weren't long out of Squamish when we saw Becca and the children in a parking area on the side of the road. Hailey and Emmett had been primed to shout encouragement and to ask if we needed water or juice. We called them our "support crew." They were surprised to see us so soon. Amid shouts of "Go Daddy, Go Grandpa," Becca hollered, "That didn't take long." They were at Shannon Falls Provincial Park—a lake-side park she'd planned to stop at and let the kids paddle and swim for a short time. I'd estimated the morning's ride would be about two hours long. Lots of time for our "support crew" to enjoy themselves.

Our late morning ride took us along the eastern shore of Howe Sound—one of the giant fiords that indent the whole of British Columbia's coastline. The Sound's major islands are Gambier and Bowen towards its western opening. But the first island you see is the eponymous Anvil Island, its rock and forest contours looking like a piece in Vulcan's forge. And, as if to emphasize the metallurgic imagery, is the actual physical presence of copper only a few kilometres before you encounter the island. That's at Britannia Beach. Now a mining museum and a national historic site, it was a thriving copper mine between 1900 and 1974. The mine and the community it engendered bounced from boom to bust, from tragedy to acts of creativity and enterprise. In 1915 for instance, 60 men, women and children were buried and killed when an avalanche crashed through the residential camp. Early in 1921 one of the mine's mills was destroyed by fire, and later that year, much of the town along the beach was swept away by an enormous flood killing 37 people. Despite this seemingly precarious existence, the company, the workers and their families built a swimming pool, tennis courts, a library and a pool hall. They mounted theatrical productions, watched movies, danced and partied. Nothing could or would prevent them from living as full a life as possible.

We rode side-by-side when the road allowed but on the long, steeper hills Daniel pulled away from me. I didn't mind.

I knew I would catch up when the road tipped downward. Even when we weren't riding together physically, I was happy knowing he was close by.

The waves of the Sound flashed in the sunlight as we pushed on. Gambier Island loomed high across the wide expanse of captured ocean. The highway dipped and swerved as it hugged the rugged coast—an engineering marvel that had taken over half a century to reach its apogee just in time for the 2010 Winter Olympics. But its history is a conflicted one and for many years the highway was considered treacherous. There have been many protests over its route and the indecisiveness on the part of politicians about improvements. For years local journalists vilified the road and the number of fatalities it had seen by renaming it the "Ski-and-Die Highway" and the "Highway of Death." With the awarding of the 2010 Winter Olympics to Vancouver and Whistler, the provincial government committed the resources to finally make the road a world-class highway which was safe, aesthetically pleasing (if that's not too much of a contradiction) and well- constructed.

Lions Bay, like the highway that passes its front door, seems precariously perched on the rock wall of Howe Sound. Side-by-side now, Daniel and I could peer over the roadside barrier down to the rows of fancy houses facing the water and the islands and Coast Mountain range beyond. It's clearly a well-heeled community ("a village" its inhabitants like to call it), and before major improvements to the highway occurred, it was susceptible to washouts and landslides caused by heavy runoff from the steep terrain above.

"A bit risky living down there." I said.

"Not these days, Dad. They've poured a lot of money into this place over the years."

"Nice pun." I quipped.

We knew we were drawing closer to Horseshoe Bay when we saw the large Langdale ferryboat heading toward the out-of-view (to us) ferry terminal. The wide, rolling and curving highway now revealed some of the engineering tricks that were used to extend the roadway out and over the shoreline below. The engineers had a great time, I'm sure, devising and calculating the mechanics involved in cantilevering the road away from the rock face in order to preserve the wall's integrity. It looked impressive.

Sailing down the off-ramp from the highway to Horseshoe Bay I knew we'd be ahead of schedule. We had ridden faster than I anticipated. Becca and the children had passed us around Lions Bay so they'd be waiting for us in the park next to the ferry terminal. And sure enough, Hailey and Emmett were jumping up and down and waving their arms in greeting as Daniel and I came into sight and pulled to a stop in front of the steps leading into the waterside park.

Joyce, Daniel's mother—my ex-wife, had come to join Becca and the children. After hugs and many photographs Grandma Joyce suggested lunch. Off we all went to sample the fish and chips Horseshoe Bay is famous for. The children seemed a little surprised when Daddy proposed an ice cream cone for dessert. Despite their insouciance, they knew they were witnessing a special occasion. But a treat as well? Parents are so unpredictable.

The three o'clock ferry to Nanaimo was running late. The children were getting a little antsy so Daniel and Becca decided the best strategy would be to say goodbye and take them home. I understood. Joyce stayed a little longer until it was time for me to join the foot passenger queue to board the ferry. Joyce and I had remained good friends after our marriage ended. Friendship was the cement of our relationship and had endured over many years despite our other relationships. That she was supportive of my ride and had come to wish me well was a typical and natural demonstration of our continued affection for one another.

The act of trundling my bike onto the BC Ferries' Horseshoe Bay to Nanaimo vessel put me into a kind of no man's land. I was neither on the Sea-to-Sky Highway nor on the Trans-Canada Highway—the road taking me from Nanaimo's Departure Bay ferry terminal south to my home in Victoria. I'd travelled this water route hundreds of times in the past and had never given a thought to its implications for a journey such as mine. What highway I was on and its name and number had been a way of defining my existence over the past weeks. Being on the ferry was a kind of interlude in that notion—a natural break in my homeward journey. I walked my bike to the back of the car deck and, after securing it, climbed the stairs to the passenger lounge. (Officially, the ferry route between Horseshoe Bay and Nanaimo is regarded as part of the Trans-Canada Highway. But that fact doesn't change how I thought and felt.)

Plunking myself down on a seat facing the rear of the boat I watched as it moved steadily from the dock into the entrance of Howe Sound and then turned west to cross the Salish Sea (formally the Georgia Strait). I looked out over the water and terrain I had just spent my morning beside and thought it amazing how far I could travel by putting one pedal in front of another in a few hours and how many places I could whiz by or people I could encounter.

I was now really heading home where I'd be surrounded by people, sights, sounds and smells that I was thoroughly familiar with—an environment that felt utterly mine. Dozing from time to time, images of the past three weeks infused my mind. Time is an illusive phenomenon that once gone can never be regained. But it can be recalled. And that's what I did. I deliberately set my mind to a particular day and went, moment-by-moment, through the events I'd experienced. Duffey Lake Road, as you might imagine, was right there. As was my first day's ride to Jake's Corner. I rode again through the low clouds and drizzle that obscured the mountains of the Spatsizi Plateau. The shimmering blackness of my first bear came vividly back. Then a spontaneous montage of faces and scenes paraded across the screen of my closed eyes. Vanora, Simpson Peak, Jackie and Jurgen, Mike and his son David, Andy and me riding beside the raging Bell-Irving River, the vast expanses of wilderness, my first view of the Fraser Canyon, even the Wee Chippie came by. On and on it went like a matinee show on the weekend. I thought of Andy and Lang and the Four Amigos and wondered how and where they were. The Four Amigos and Lang, along with Christian and Adrian, had, by now, experienced the ride down Vancouver Island to Nanaimo. They had ridden through my own back-yard. Perhaps they'd travelled on this same ferryboat—going the other way.

Drawing near to Nanaimo's Departure Bay ferry terminal I envisioned Lorinda and Mia waiting at the arrivals gate with people I'd never met before. I'd last seen Lorinda less than a month ago when she had driven me to the airport on a warm, bright July morning. "Goodbye my love. I know you'll have a wonderful time. You always do." I caught my breath as I slid from her arms. "I will. Talk to you soon—from Whitehorse." Now it was early August and I was almost home. The dewy-eyes of parting would be those of greeting as we embraced each other again.

Mia had been busy since I last saw her. She'd been in regular contact with Betty Hum of Parkinson Society BC and had helped arrange for my stays in Prince George with Mike and Valerie and in Squamish, via Ursula and then Leslie, at the retirement residence. When I first told her of my proposed journey a year earlier she'd immediately suggested she'd write a Facebook Page. I had no idea what a Facebook Page was or how they were initiated, written or read. "Don't worry Dad. It's easy. It's like a blog. Lots of people will like it. This way people who donate to your fundraiser can follow your progress." In typical fashion, she concluded our short discussion about the work involved by saying. "Anyway Dad, it'll be fun."

I hadn't read any of Mia's blog while on the road but she always gave me snippets of what she'd posted and some of people's comments and words of encouragement during our frequent phone conversations. In a few paragraphs she seemed to capture the essence of the few days' rides I'd described to her. I could hear her infectious humour and her genuine enthusiasm for life in almost every sentence she read even though it was my experiences she was writing of. She confessed that it was more work than she'd thought but she was really enjoying our conversations, the writing and the positive responses (the "like") from all kinds of people.

I could see a small bevy of people gathered on the other side of a metal fence as I made for the gate that was the bicycle exit from the terminal. Lorinda and Mia were waving and calling me over. "John, it's this way," shouted Lorinda. The "small bevy" were members of the Nanaimo Parkinson's support group. They were making their own sounds. Along with cheers of greeting, two were ringing hand bells while one man was playing a mandolin. A few were holding small banners with the word "Freeze!" written in bold letters across the top. This was a reference to bradykinesia or slowness of movement that is one of the most wretched of symptoms that Parkinson's sufferers experience.

Amongst all the excitement and chatter I was aware of the man playing the mandolin. He was introduced to me as Marv. Of all the folks I'd met with Parkinson's disease, his symptoms seemed the most extreme and visible. But despite the physical contortions of his face, hands and legs he was able to play his mandolin, engage in conversation and ride his three-wheeled bike. Before we all left the terminal for a nearby pub and restaurant, Marv came up to me and, in a faltering voice, offered to meet Lorinda and me next morning and escort us out of town. I told him it would be a fitting departure from Nanaimo and we agreed to meet in front of our hotel at 8:30 the next morning. With that arrangement made, he cycled off, away from the direction we were all headed.

I was ecstatic to see Lorinda again and to have her near me. We held and squeezed hands as we sat side-by-side at an outside table on the pub's sun deck. Across the table Mia was being her relaxed and effervescent self. From the way she interacted with the Nanaimo group and knew all their names it was clear she'd been arranging this welcome for some time. A woman named Janet was sitting next to me. Her husband had been diagnosed with the disease a number of years ago and took early retirement because of it. She talked of what life was like living with Parkinson's—for the sufferer and for the caregiver. Money was a big one. The governments, federal and provincial, weren't really responsive to the needs of the patient or their caregivers. Nor were they investing in research. That's why, she said, public awareness was so important if change was to happen. She touched my arm and said in an earnest tone, "Us carrying those Freeze banners; that wasn't a protest but our way of bringing attention to the disease." Another woman shushed the table to attention. In her hand was a cheque, which she handed to me. It was the group's donation to my fundraising effort. As in Prince George, I was surprised and touched. The generosity of spirit displayed by this group of sufferers and their spouses put my journey into perspective. I was enjoying myself. My only burden was my two panniers. These folks were stuck with either an incurable disease, or caring for someone who had, this day and for the rest of their lives.

Lorinda and Mia drove to the downtown hotel we'd booked for the night while I rode there on my bike. The front desk clerk was aware of who we were and was completely accommodating when I asked to keep my and Lorinda's bike in our room. Later that evening, after Mia had left to visit friends, Lorinda and I walked hand in hand to our favourite Nanaimo restaurant—Gina's. It's a Mexican restaurant that we've been going to for years. The atmosphere was relaxed and the food good and plentiful. Being with my wife again, eating and sipping our cervezas, was enough to make me feel totally content and was the perfect end to a day when I'd embraced my whole family and made them part of a journey that was almost at its end.

Nanaimo to Victoria (110 km)

6 The Trans-Canada Highway (Highway 1)
Nanaimo to Victoria

Day 25 Nanaimo to Victoria

This was it. My last day on the road. And I would be riding with my wife—my lovely lady (as I often refer to her). Since the beginning of our relationship we've enjoyed being outdoors together. The closeness and emotional bond that exists between us is always enriched and sharpened when we're riding or hiking or just strolling with each other. Today would be no different.

Outside the lobby of our hotel Marv was waiting. On reflection, he'd decided not to escort us out of town. Listening closely to what he was saying, he thought he'd be too slow and be a nuisance. He didn't want to get in the way. That wouldn't be the case I told him, we weren't in a hurry. He insisted and we parted. I watched him pedal away. It seemed like work for him and I knew he'd made the right decision.

I felt a little sheepish as I began my day's ride, once again, without my panniers. Lorinda was on her light road bike and the only sensible way for us to ride together was to make my bike lighter. I loaded the panniers into Mia's car outside the hotel and arranged to meet her 10 kilometres north of Victoria at four o'clock.

To get out of town and onto the Trans-Canada Highway Lorinda and I made our way to Haliburton Street, a quiet side road marked as a designated cycling route. At 8:30 in the morning there was no traffic to speak of and we were able to ease into our day's ride with this gentle detour skirting a longish climb that's on the main road leaving the city.

I felt a palpable tingle running through me while riding beside Lorinda along this back road of Nanaimo. My journey was almost over and I was only a 100 kilometres from completing one of the most rewarding challenges I'd ever set for myself. Though I'd never really doubted my body's or my mind's ability to accomplish the journey I still couldn't quite believe I'd covered almost 2,500 kilometres in 21 days of riding.

We joined the Trans-Canada about half-a-kilometre from its junction with the Nanaimo Parkway—a long four-lane highway that bypasses the city on its west side. I could see it would be by far the most interesting merging of traffic of my whole trip. At the junction Lorinda and I, with eyes peeled, maneuvered our bikes across two lanes of merging southbound traffic coming off the bypass and then, after another 500 metres, back across two lanes of speeding vehicles as the highway split into two separate roadways—one keeping south (the one we wanted), the other going right to the Duke Point ferry terminal. It was a bit hair-raising but we kept our wits about us and came to no harm. I've always maintained that to be safe in traffic a cyclist must ride offensively giving clear hand signals, being aware of what's around all the time, and making eye contact with drivers as much as possible. The latter, I'll admit, is sometime hard to do when a vehicle is travelling in excess of 80 kph!

There are few countries in the world that have a national highway as long as Canada's. While Australia's Highway 1 and the Trans-Siberian Highway are longer, ours is still over 8,000-kilometres long (8,030 to be exact.) and travels from coast to coast through all ten provinces. It would be considered uninterrupted were it not for bodies of water near both ends (or starts)—the Salish Sea between BC's mainland and Vancouver Island and the Gulf of St. Lawrence between Nova Scotia and Newfoundland.

Just to let you know that despite my snide comment about Whistler's inclusion of "Bienvenue" on its welcome sign, I do appreciate that we live in a bilingual country and often prefer the French language's more poetic-sounding name for things. *Route Transcanadienne* is one of them. Why say "Trans-Canada Highway" when you could use the much more mellifluous *"Route Transcanadienne?"*

The Trans-Canada Highway becomes Douglas Street as it enters Victoria and continues to its western terminus at "Mile O" at the very end of Douglas as it meets the ocean at the foot of Beacon Hill Park. Lorinda's office is on Douglas Street in downtown. I had my office kitty-corner to hers on the same street. Neither of us has ever thought of ourselves working along the Trans-Canada—the nation's premier thoroughfare. But she does and I did. We'd been working on its sidewalk for years. To think of the highway like that takes away some of the romanticism of riding along the "national highway."

Today's ride would bring back some of the road's glamour. As I wrote before about my ferry crossing, the name of the highway I was on helped define my journey; oriented me as to where I'd come from and where I was headed; gave meaning to the kilometres I'd covered. Now I was on my sixth highway—the Trans-Canada Highway (even though I'd only be riding a fraction of its length).

Running due south the highway is never far away from the coves, bays, inlets and islands of the Salish Sea. Nearly always, if you look left, you see water and, if you can't see that, the Cascade Mountains are there rising as a glorious backdrop. And if you know where to look and it's a clear day, Mt. Baker sits tall and sedate in the far off southeast.

Ladysmith is a quiet little town on the upside of the highway. It was our first stop of the day. The hillside town is built directly on the 49th parallel (the same latitude as Paris!) and had its beginnings in 1898 as a coal port built by James Dunsmuir, the notorious coal baron of Vancouver Island. Needing housing for the families of the men working his mines just south of Nanaimo, he developed the hill above the port as a small town. Dunsmuir named the town to honour the British defeat of the Boers in the battle of Ladysmith in South Africa. It's a quaint place with one main street lined with early 20th century buildings—mostly stores. The highway skirts the town centre on the waterside and you look down on the Transfer Beach Park that was once the port and across Ladysmith Harbour.

Not long after we started riding again Lorinda got a flat. I couldn't believe it. I'd just covered almost 2,500 kilometres and hadn't one puncture and here's Lorinda, after less than

30 with a flat tire. It was her rear wheel—always the most awkward. We found a wide spot on the shoulder of the highway—out of harm's way, and I set to work changing the inner tube. It's often an ego thing—changing the tube—mostly among guys. How fast you can accomplish the task can lead to a feather in your cap. Joe, a friend of ours, has changed a flat in a minute. He has a number of feathers. On group rides everyone defers to Joe with punctures. I took my time and we were on our way after about ten minutes.

We crossed the Chemainus River on a long girder bridge and stopped at a favourite farmer's market—Russell's—to buy some fruit. The market is at the junction with Mt. Sicker Road—a road leading to the ferry terminals for Thetis and Penelakut islands as well as to Salt Spring Island via Crofton. All three islands are part of the Gulf Islands—a large archipelago that scatters its islands into the Salish Sea between Vancouver Island, the Lower Mainland and Washington State. (The American San Juan Islands to the south are part of the same archipelago.) A twenty-minute break was enough to finish our fruit and be back on our bikes. We planned to have lunch in Duncan, a town halfway between Nanaimo and Victoria.

The signage for the Trans-Canada Highway is a white maple leaf on a green background and is ubiquitous along its length. Despite that constant reminder many Vancouver Islanders refer to the road as simply the Island Highway. A logical name if ever there was one. Entering Duncan we were greeted by a large sign telling us it was the "City of Totems." Throughout the town are dozens of tall, colourful and skillfully detailed totem poles each hand-carved by Cowichan First Nation carvers. The Cowichan Tribe are a dynamic Coast Salish people and own and operate a number of successful businesses in the community that once included the Cherry Point Vineyards—an award winning and very respected winery on the island. No, the highway doesn't pass the vineyards but they're not far away.

We bought tasty bean and quinoa salads at a take-out deli and sat in the shade to eat. It was sunny and warm, ideal weather for riding. We were making good time but the ride from Duncan to Victoria would be the stiffest of the day with the Malahat Drive awaiting us before descending to our rendezvous with Mia. The long climb out of Duncan put space between Lorinda and me. I couldn't stay with her even when I got out of the saddle. The four lanes of the highway began to feel like a racetrack as the road flattened. Cars and trucks whizzing by as if this admittedly uninteresting portion of the highway was an inducement to drivers to push the 90kph speed limit. We kept well out of trouble on the wide shoulder.

The Malahat announces its presence in two ways: by a roadside sign reading "Start Malahat Drive"; and by a long intimidating rise that disappears over a hump further up the road. It starts just outside of Mill Bay, a small town 30 kilometres north of Victoria. It's an up-and-over section of the highway and lasts about 20 kilometres. But what 20 kilometres they are.

All roads have a history and the Malahat's stretches well over a hundred years. In the late 1800s the only route between the Cowichan Valley (50-odd kilometres north of Victoria) and Victoria was a rambling wagon road that followed a bumpy route through the hills west of the Malahat. The settlers of the valley relied heavily on weekly steamship deliveries to Victoria for their supplies and farmers needed to get their produce to market there. This inland route was too arduous and long. The valley people hated it. They petitioned the government to build a quicker route on the eastern flank of the Malahat, a road that would travel along the edge of the Saanich Inlet and Finlayson Arm. The first surveyors said it couldn't be done. Too difficult—a waste of money to even try. That was in 1874. It took a provincial election and a petition with hundreds of signatures twenty-nine years later, to prod a new government, in 1903, to start work on a shorter road. It was finished in 1911.

In a little over a century, the Malahat Drive has gone from a rough, single lane gravel road without guard rails—one that took courage and skill to negotiate, to being one of the most scenic parts of the Trans-Canada Highway. But, like the Sea-to-Sky Highway I rode yesterday, it can be a dangerous and deadly road to travel. People are killed and maimed every year on its smooth pavement and, like a hundred years ago, still needs skill to negotiate whenever the weather turns rotten.

We'd stopped in Mill Bay to replenish our water bottles—we wanted to make sure we stayed hydrated for the hard work ahead. Back on the road I suggested Lorinda take the lead and not wait for me. If we got too gapped we would re-form at the Spectacle Lake turn-off, just beyong the summit. The first pitch is deceptive. It doesn't seem much but after about 400 metres you start to work hard—harder than you want.

I kept Lorinda within a few metres most of the way up the first kilometre climb but when the road ramped up to 8% she pulled away. The four lanes out of Mill Bay had now narrowed into three as the highway started to cling to the steep rock face of the mountain. On the left was the Split Rock Lookout drive-through that was separated from the roadway by a huge rock the size of a couple of two-story houses. The drive-through is a vestige of the original road before the mountain was blasted away to make the road wider and safer. I didn't stop to take in the view, mainly because it's illegal to make a left turn across the highway at this point, but also, I was still climbing and didn't want to break my rhythm. Cycling and driving north I'd stopped many times and knew the panoramic scene well. The viewpoint looks over the Saanich peninsula and, to the left, Salt Spring Island and other Gulf Islands behind. To see the peninsula spread out before you like a giant topographical map is quite dramatic. You look down on a fascinating quilt of human settlement with farmland here, forested and rocky terrain there, clusters of houses set amongst the trees everywhere, some industrial and commercial buildings, Victoria airport, the town of Sidney way on the far side, and all of it encircled by a long, gracefully-curving coastline.

I arrived at the summit with Lorinda nowhere in sight. She'd obviously taken me at my word and pushed on to the turn-off. At 352 metres (1,154 ft) the Malahat summit is not one of the highest points on the Trans-Canada by a long shot, but it's still a good climb and has a nice reward—a great view across the Saanich Inlet to the domed hills of Gowlland Tod Provincial Park. I got a sightseer to take a photograph of me with the hills in the background and then rode on to catch Lorinda. It only took a few minutes to join her and then we readied ourselves for the long and swift descent. Lorinda's a good descender and enjoys a fast downhill. But not the Malahat. For her it's too hairy. She doesn't like the rumble strip, the traffic, the noise, (and other things besides, which I'll get to). So it was decided I should lead. I would be in my element. If I got too far ahead, I'd wait for her at the entrance to Goldstream Park—the south end of the Drive.

The trouble with roads like the Malahat, ones that cut

through stone and rock and cling close to the rock face, is there tends to be lots of debris on the shoulder. You always have to keep your eyes open for fallen rock and shards in your path. Although the highway's maintenance crews try to keep the Malahat's shoulders clear, there's always some rubble on the ground. It's also puncture territory. Travelling at 60-plus kph you don't want one. (See why Lorinda doesn't like descending this road?) Knowing this about the road makes you cautious—in control but wary. And that's how we descended the Malahat.

For me, the most spectacular stretch of the Malahat going south is the sweeping, left-hand downhill into Goldstream Provincial Park. You're close to the rock face for sure, but on the left, across Finlayson Arm, rises the gnarly northwest face of Mt. Finlayson. If you dare to look, it's in your sights the whole way down. It's a favourite climb of mine. Non-technical but interesting, it has a few ledges and a narrow chimney near the top. It's only 419 metres (1,374 ft) high and takes about half-an-hour to climb.

Despite Lorinda's apprehension about riding down the Malahat, this day she had no problem staying on my wheel. Every few minutes I'd glance over my shoulder to see how far she'd fallen back. But no, she was right behind me.

We cruised through Goldstream Park, its giant cedar and spreading maple trees keeping the road in their shade. Whenever I'm in Goldstream Park or passing through I always think of Emily Carr. This would be the second time on my trip she'd come to mind. Carr was fascinated by trees; big, tall, slender trees—cedars especially. She'd been encouraged in her work and vision by Lawren Harris and by the impact of the Group of Seven. In 1933 she bought a small trailer, "The Elephant" she called it, and converted it into a mobile studio. The first place she took it was Goldstream Flats—a place close to where the Goldstream River enters Finlayson Arm—a lovely part of the park. She camped out (her bathtub was the shallow waters of the estuary) and took walks into the surrounding forest and painted what she saw. Her vision.

The road tilted up again at the park's south end. It was the last hill that stood in our way before we left the highway to meet Mia. The distance between the park and where she was waiting was less than five kilometres. But it was a four-lane highway again. It was also Friday afternoon—the busiest time for traffic. Despite all the noise of the cars and trucks roaring by, despite running the gauntlet at every off- and on-ramp we had to cross, I was happy. I was on home turf and was surrounded by names and sights that told me I had returned. I floated down the exit ramp with Lorinda close behind. A quick right and then left and we were with Mia at the Atkins Road access to the Galloping Goose Regional Trail—a trail that travels 55 kilometres from the Sooke Hills all the way into Victoria. We were an hour early.

Almost the last thing I'd said to Mia before we parted that morning in Nanaimo was, "Can't be exact about the time we'll get to the Goose, so you might want to be there before four." I was glad to see her waiting.

Lorinda, Mia and I were in good spirits as we relaxed on the bench under an awning beside the trail. Being a regional trail, well used and maintained, it had a few access points that provided parking, toilets, a bench and a large, covered trail-system map. Atkins Road was one of them

"I should get going. You do know you can't get to the Switch Bridge before five Dad. In fact you and Lorinda have to be really on time. Not before, not after." I knew Mia was planning something special and I knew it was where the trail crossed over the Trans-Canada Highway on the pedestrian/bike-only bridge—the Switch Bridge. She is the consummate organizer and surprise expert. I didn't want to foul things up. We unloaded my panniers from her car and I put them on my bike. There was no way I was going to ride into Victoria without my full load. Besides, what would people say? I'd been dogging it?"

I'd estimated the 10-kilometre ride along the Goose would take about 25 to 30 minutes—it was dead flat and paved. "We'll make good time and be on time," I assured Mia before she drove away. Waiting about 10 minutes after Mia left Lorinda and I set off.

Pedalling on the Goose I felt good. My body showed no signs of fatigue or distress. I had no injuries or aches. Had no sore spots! I had the same pleasure of feeling the warmth of the sun on my arms and my legs turning loose circles riding toward Victoria as I had on my first day's ride out of Whitehorse.

The Switch Bridge came into view some two hundred metres away. I can't deny I was excited about my journey's end and that I was expecting to see some friends who Mia had invited to welcome me home at the Bridge. (She's told me that much.) Close to the Bridge Lorinda dropped back. It came closer and closer and then, rounding the bend to its ramp, I couldn't believe my eyes.

Balloons, banners, smiling faces, waving arms held high, voices loud with cheering—all were welcoming me back home. Spread across the trail were friends, acquaintances and people I'd never seen before—all them gathered together in greeting. Mia was the first to hug me. "Welcome home, Dad. You did awesome." I was on the edge of tears as friend after friend hugged me. I had a strong but different bond with each of them. People I hardly knew shook my hand. I was introduced to a man who suffered from Parkinson's. "Thank you John. What you've done is amazing. We all appreciate it." Someone put a glass of champagne in my hand and the cheer went up—"Welcome home."

I find it hard to remember all that happened in the next hour or so. I was so overwhelmed by the warmth and support of the people who'd welcomed me back that late afternoon. Mia had done "her thing," as she would say, in organizing it all. After a brief interview with a local radio host, Lorinda and I tied a bunch of balloons to each of our bikes and set off home.

Riding through the streets of Victoria with balloons bobbing in my draft it seemed an impossibly short time since I was last here, since I'd dismantled my bike, flown with it to Whitehorse, put it back together again and ridden home. But what I'd done, where I'd been and what I'd seen over the past three-and-a-half weeks were already filtering their way into my memory bank. The beauty of memory is, although we can't ever rewind our experiences in real time, we can come close through our memories and our imagination. The experiences may be gone but they're not lost. And though I knew I could never repeat my journey I also knew that it would stay with me forever. It would be part of who I am and, even in my early seventies, who I would become.

Epilogue

When all the donations were counted by Parkinson Society British Columbia (PSBC) in early September, the total amount I'd raised came to just under $13,000. I was amazed. Given where my expectations were at the beginning of June when I first spoke to Betty Hum (when I confessed to fearing I wouldn't raise a cent) and what I actually achieved was a mile of difference. My thanks and gratitude to all who contributed was immense, and still is.

As of today, no cure has been found for Parkinson's even though it's one of the world's most pervasive and insidious neurological diseases. No researcher, no clinician, no doctor has discovered a way to prevent or slow, let alone cure, the disease. Canada has over 100,000 of its citizens suffering from Parkinson's and 11,000 live in BC. (There are more than a million in the US and 10 million worldwide.)

For those who know little or nothing of Parkinson's, here's what it looks like: The trouble starts in the midbrain, in the substantia nigra, where the neurotransmitter dopamine is produced. Dopamine smoothes out nerve impulses as they move from nerve cell to nerve cell—cells that transmit messages to the body's muscles to initiate voluntary movement. When dopamine production is impaired, i.e. falls below 50%, the classic Parkinson's symptoms arise. Smoothness of movement disappears. Muscles are overtaken by shaking, rigidity, slowness and stiffness. Walking and balance become difficult. Shuffling becomes a way of staying upright. The clarity and volume of speech diminishes. Handwriting becomes illegible.

Nephew Richard is one of a growing number of younger people being diagnosed with Parkinson's. PSBC estimates that 40% of new cases are diagnosed before the age of 60; many are as young as 30. Richard is doing much better these days. He's now on a cocktail of drugs including levadopa, the medication of choice in the world of Parkinson's and his symptoms are more stable. (Even he would appreciate the pun.) On a visit to England last summer we had hiked together—in the rain.

The Sunday after my return I got a phone call from Andy. He'd arrived in Vancouver and wondered if he could take up my invitation to visit on his way to Seattle. I was delighted. Of course he could come. "Stay as long as you want," I told him. He stayed for a couple of days, sightseeing and just hanging out. I rode with him to the Coho ferry terminal in Victoria's Inner Harbour and saw him off. The last time I heard from Andy was from Antigua in Guatemala in December of 2012. He'd just ridden from the Canadian border down the western states, through the Baja and the Mexican mainland to Guatemala. A journey of 7,493 kilometres (4,656 miles in his currency) he completed in 111 days. There remains a long way to go to reach Tierra del Fuego. But he still has lots of years of riding in him. I somehow know he'll make it.

Mia deemed her Facebook Page of my journey a success. She'd thoroughly enjoyed writing it as I'd enjoyed recounting my life on the road to her every couple of days. Well over a 100 people had "liked" her daily postings (she'd also written a page on the days we hadn't talked) most of which sent me words of support and encouragement in return. Her "page" was titled *John's Ride for Parkinson's* and she called her postings "Report from the Road." "One thing I really liked," she told me days after my return, "was getting to respond and chat with so many neat people. People I'd never heard of as well as those I knew but only vaguely. It was fun!" Although it was more work than she'd thought, she's learned much about her home province than she otherwise would. She also got to be part of my ride's logistics—helping to organize my accommodations and media interviews. I was happy knowing she'd been part of my journey.

I recovered well from my long ride. By the end of August Lorinda and I were cycling in the flat lands of southern Alberta between visits to Lorinda's parents. In early September, I was hiking in the Grand Tetons of Wyoming with my good friend and hiking buddy Brian. When the weather turned crappy we drove on to Utah and hiked in the glorious sandstone mountains and canyons of Zion National Park.

One of the keys to long distance endeavours, whether cycling, running or hiking, is not to over extend yourself. Keep the pace steady—your own pace, not someone else's. It's a lesson I've learned over many years of training and racing. That's not to say I haven't made any errors in judging my body's capabilities—I have. I've dropped out of two marathons because I started too fast. I've over trained and been injured many times. I still make mistakes. My mind has often outperformed my body in what it thinks my body can do. Listening to your body is one thing; deciphering what it has to say is something different. It takes time, patience and a good deal of reflection on past experiences to pick up its signals and anticipate what it can and cannot do. When we're feeling our best is often the time we're the most vulnerable; when we're on the edge of our physical precipice. One false step—too far, too long or too hard—and we're over the edge, injured, fatigued or become ill—or all three.

The challenge I face, as I grow older, is the constant search for the evolving boundary of my body's capabilities. With each passing year my aerobic capacity diminishes. I can no longer run, ride or hike as fast I did only a few years ago. I'm not as strong as I once was—I don't volunteer to help people move house any more. The one aspect of my physical abilities that stays relatively stable is going long—my endurance. I can still do those century rides. But each year, each month even, I have to reassess what my body can do and tailor my training accordingly. Over the past ten years, I've curtailed my workouts from six days a week to three. That's not to imply I do nothing on the other four days. I go for walks almost every day. As you read in my account of my journey home from Whitehorse, I was determined not to over extend myself. I didn't try to keep up with the four young Mexicans. Andy rode with me on his easy days. I climbed the hills playing out my energy as the slope steepened. I always knew that to finish my ride wanting to do more, I had to be patient and content and aware of what my body could do.

The following summer (2012), I went with an old friend of mine, Leo, on an eight-day bike tour of southwestern BC. We cycled a large loop from Victoria, up the Fraser Canyon to Lillooet and back to Victoria via Whistler and Nanaimo. And yes, we rode the Duffey Lake Road. Up that "God damn hill," as Leo would later refer to it. The climb was just as I remembered it—difficult, challenging and just as satisfying reaching the top. And the battle between my mind's mind and my body's mind raged again. Will I embark on another long, demanding and spectacular journey again? Depends how this body of mine holds up—how well I take care of it. And... if my mind can persuade it to do more than it thinks it can. I'll wait and see. But I do have plans.

Well, a plan did materialize. In the summer of 2014, two months after the first printing of this book, I set off to cycle from Victoria down the coasts of Washington, Oregon and northern California to attend a friend's sixty-fifth birthday celebration in San Francisco. I covered 1,744 kilometres in 15 days of riding. Although I suffered up many long and steep hills, I didn't walk and arrived safely (and in good shape to party).

Appendices

1. My equipment: the bike; panniers; tent.
2. My itinerary with distance, riding time and average speed.
3. Where I stayed.

Appendix 1

My equipment

The bike

The bike I chose for my journey was not the typical touring bike. My three primary needs in a bike were: lightness; mountain bike-type gearing, i.e. easy; straight handlebars. Luckily, I found that combination in Mountain Equipment Co-op's Shadowlands—a bike they refer to as a commuter/weekend-touring bike. Here are some of its specifications:

Weight—11.9kgs (22.3lbs)
Frame—aluminum
Forks—carbon
Seatpost—carbon
Brakes—disc
Cranks + rings—Shimano Deore 48-36-26
Rear derailleur—Shimano SLX Shadow
Cassette—Shimano Deore 10-speed 11-34
Pedals—Crank Brothers Candy 3 (egg beaters)
Tires—Continental Touring Plus (700´32)
Saddle—Selle Royal Viper.

I had tested two bona-fide touring bikes just to feel how they rode (I'd always toured on a non-suspension mountain bike) and to make sure my intuition and preferences were right. The gearing was definitely not easy enough and the drop handlebars were a redundancy for me (I have them on my road bike but I'm rarely in the drops) as an upright position is more comfortable when I'm riding long distances with panniers.

I also like the brakes and gear shifters to be integral to bar handgrips—as they are with straight handlebars.

The moment I mounted and rode the Shadowlands I knew I was on the bike I wanted. It was light; had a smooth feel; the handlebars were at the right height and distance from the saddle; the shifters and brake levers were in the ideal position; the saddle felt comfortable; the pedals were easy to clip in and out. In short, I had found my perfect bike.

Panniers

I had bought a pair of Axion, Journey Series panniers in 2008 and had used them a few times. I had them as I toured both the Gulf Islands and the San Juan Island—once with my wife, other times alone. They were with me the year before my Whitehorse to Victoria ride as I cycled a circular route around Washington State.

At 45 litres carrying capacity (that's about 50lbs of stuff) I found them adequate for my needs. They have side and back pockets and, while not waterproof, came with a set of waterproof yellow covers. Over the times of use they have withstood dozens of packing and unpacking, hooking and unhooking, leaning against trees and fences and the odd brush with the gravel surface of a back road.

Hooked either side of my rack the panniers left plenty of room for me to utilize the rack's platform. There I bungy-corded a large waterproof stuff sack containing my tent, Therm-a-Rest and sleeping bag (all double wrapped in plastic to ensure they stayed dry).

The tent

My obsession with lightweight gear drew me to a tent the store manager of my sponsor, Capital Iron, suggested. It was a Big Agnes Fly Creek UL2—an ultra-light (UL) two person tent that weighed 2lbs 10 ozs. With a footprint (ground sheet) it weighed 3lbs. (They now make them even lighter.) Although it was a snug two-person affair, it was just the right size to accommodate two panniers, my handlebar bag and me.

Appendix 2

My itinerary with distance, riding time and average speed

Day		
1	Whitehorse – Jake's Corner	82 km; 5 hrs:30 mins; 15 kph
2	Jake's Corner – Teslin	99 km; 5 hrs:28 mins; 18 kph
3	Teslin – Walker's Lodge	125 km; 7 hrs:11 mins; 17 kph
4	Walker's Lodge – Nugget City	114 km
5	Nugget City – Boya Lake Prov. Park	90 km; 5 hrs:23 mins; 16.7 kph
6	Boya Lake – Dease Lake	144 km (122 km riding)
7	Rest Day	
8	Dease Lake – Tatogga	100 km; 6 hrs:21 mins; 15.1 kph
9	Tatogga – Bell II	143 km; 9 hrs;11 mins; 15.1 kph
10	Bell II – Meziadin Prov. Park	96 km; 6 hrs:12 mins; 15.4 kph
11	Meziadin – Kitwanga	154 km; 9 hrs:26 mins; 16.4 kph
12	Kitwanga – Smithers	119 km; 7 hrs:23 mins; 16.1 kph
13	Rest Day	
14	Smithers – Burns Lake	149 km; 8 hrs:33 mins; 17.4 kph
15	Burns Lake – Vanderhoof	132 km; 7 hrs:05 mins; 18.7 kph
16	Vanderhoof – Prince George	110 km; 5 hrs:45 mIns; 19 kph
17	Rest Day	
18	Prince George – Quesnel	125 km; 7 hrs:25 mins; 16.8 kph
19	Quesnel – Williams Lake	122 km; 6 hrs:49 mins; 17.9 kph
20	Williams Lake – 70 Mile House	132 km; 7 hrs:17 mins; 18.1 kph
21	70 Mile House – Lillooet	140 km; 7 hrs:19 mins; 19 kph
22	Lillooet – Pemberton	109 km; 6 hrs:49 mins; 15.7 kpm
23	Pemberton – Squamish	107 km; 6hrs:49 mins; 15.7 kph
24	Squamish – Nanaimo	45 km; 2 hrs:00 mins; 20.7 kph
25	Nanaimo – Victoria	110 km; 5 hrs+; 19.5 kph
	Total:	**2,547 km**

Appendix 3

Where I stayed:

Whitehorse – Vanora's home

Jake's Corner – Gas Bar and Restaurant. Tel: 867.399.3200

Teslin – Yukon Motel's campground. Tel: 869.390.2443

Walker's Continental Divide Lodge's campground.
Tel: 867.851.6451

Nugget City – Nugget City Cabins. Tel: 867.536.2307

Boya Lake Provincial Park, Highway 37.

Dease Lake – Campground and Northway Motor Inn.
Tel: 250.771.5341

Tatogga – Tatogga Lake Resort. Tel: 250.234.3526

Bell II – Lodge and Campground. Tel: 250.275.4770

Kitwanga – Cassiar RV Park. Tel: 250.849.5799

Smithers – Jackie's home

Burns Lake – Traveller's Motel. Tel: 250.692.7471

Vanderhoof – Riverside Park Campground. Tel: 250.567.4710

Prince George – Mike and Valerie's home.

Quesnel – Fraser River Bridge Inn. Tel: 250.992.5860

70 Mile House – 70 Mile Motel. Tel: 250.456.7500

Lillooet – 4 Pines Motel. Tel: 250.256.4247

Pemberton – Marcia and Bob's home/garden

Squamish – Retirement residence

Nanaimo – Coast Bastion Hotel. Tel: 250.753.6601

THE AUTHOR

John Crouch is a well-known Victoria author. His three guidebooks, *Walk Victoria, Hike Victoria* and *Bike Victoria* are local best sellers.

John has cycled, hiked, climbed and run most of his life. As a competitive masters athlete he has been national champion in both the triathlon and duathlon. He has also completed 16 marathons and won his age category in five of them.

Since turning sixty he has climbed Mt. Baker, Mt. Whitney (twice) and Vancouver Island's highest peak, the Golden Hinde. He has hiked extensively in the UK, Europe, California and the deserts of southwestern United States.

His recent long-distance bike tours include: a 1,400-km circle of Washington State; a 1,100-km, five-day supported ride on Highway 3 from Coleman, Alberta to Victoria, BC and an 800-km circle from Victoria to Victoria via the Fraser Canyon and the Sea-to-Sky Highway.

Believe it or not, despite his abiding enthusiasm for the outdoors, John enjoys spending time at home with his wife and visiting with his children, his grandchildren and his friends.